The ANSWER BOOK
for Parents of Teenagers

KATHLEEN YAPP

BARBOUR
PUBLISHING, INC.
Uhrichsville, Ohio

The
ANSWER
BOOK

for Parents
of
Teenagers

Published by Barbour Publishing, Inc., P. O. Box 719, Uhrichsville, Ohio 44683 http://www.barbourbooks.com

Member of the
Evangelical Christian
Publishers Association

Printed in the United States of America.

Acknowledgments

To the dozens of men and women who shared their parental insight with me—*Thanks*, and my prayers are with you.

Dedication

To my children, Lisa, David, Terry, and Jim, who gave me the knowledge and experience to write this book, and to my "everything's under control" husband, Ken, who raised them with me and still found time to be my best friend—*Thanks* to all, with hugs and undying love.

Contents

Introduction

During an interview for this book, one mother revealed, "I've wanted children, or rather, babies, ever since I was five years old." Then she sighed. "But I never said I wanted teenagers."

Having raised four teenagers myself—and still being alive to tell the story—I understood exactly what she meant. Something mysterious happens at age thirteen to these darlings we yearn for, give birth to, raise with loving attention, and expect to take care of us when we become old and infirm: They become teenagers.

If you've ever despaired over your teenage son's cavalier attitude toward alcohol, drugs, and smoking, or wondered why your previously sweet, compliant daughter now constantly battles your authority, *The Answer Book* will introduce you to other parents who are going through the same situations (and more). They have graciously consented to share what they're doing to cope with such crises.

If you have decided to board up your child's messy room, are afraid to bring up the subject of sex, despair over his rebellious attitude toward church, and haven't a clue how to get her to be responsible about chores and money, this book will give you specific answers to specific problems.

Whatever the struggle you're having with your

teenager, just turn to the appropriate chapter and find twenty or so suggestions from other parents, the real "experts" when it comes to child raising.

My four teenagers are adults now. The miracle is that we're still speaking and, in fact, love and respect each other and enjoy being together.

It is possible to raise children through their teen years and survive. By trusting first in the wisdom of God and praying for His patience in dealing with your children, you will find a way through the maze of confusion that surrounds the years thirteen through nineteen.

Don't run away from home! Read a few chapters of *The Answer Book* and then smile. You're not alone. God loves you.

Kathleen Yapp

ALCOHOL, DRUGS, AND SMOKING

Do you not know that you are the temple of God and that the Spirit of God dwells in you? If anyone defiles the temple of God, God will destroy him. For the temple of God is holy, which temple you are.

1 CORINTHIANS 3:16,17

I have a thing about orange juice: Kids need it for breakfast. The perfect jumpstart for the day, orange juice helps them see better, move faster, smile sweeter, and get straight As. This amazing breakfast elixir even gives kids a cooperative attitude that brings parents, teachers, and friends to their knees in appreciation.

"Girls admire boys who drink orange juice," I told my sons many times with tongue in cheek. "Boys think girls are cool who have orange juice with breakfast," I told my daughter.

There was a reason why all four children had an annoying habit of rolling their eyes when I made those comments: They had not yet had their daily dose of orange juice; in other words, they were not yet cooperative and understanding!

But then came the day I served grape juice instead.

"What's this?" Terry bellowed. Since he was the oldest, he had the best bellow.

"Will I throw up if I drink it?" our youngest son David asked.

"My complexion will be a mess today without my orange juice, Mom," Lisa wailed.

Only Jim had the maturity not to make a silly comment. He held the glass to his mouth and took a deep swallow. We all watched for his reaction.

"It tastes just like wine," he announced, a superior look of awareness covering his face. At the age of fourteen he thought of himself already as a connoisseur.

"Wine?" the other three kids screeched.

"Wine?" I questioned in a tone meant to remind our second oldest child that we lived in an alcohol-free home. "Where have you tasted wine?" I asked. Hands found their way to the hips. Eyebrows were appropriately raised.

Jim stared at me. I stared back.

"Mr. Lowell gave me some," he finally admitted.

"Mr. Lowell?"

"My friend Danny's father. You know Danny?"

"Yes, I do. But why would Mr. Lowell give two young

boys wine to drink?"

"Because we asked him. He was having some, and we wanted to know what it tasted like."

"Didn't he protest?"

"It was just a sip. It didn't hurt anything."

I let out a deep breath. "Every journey starts with that first step."

"But I don't even know if I'll start that journey," he countered, and then his expression became serious. "If I do, it will be my own choice. Your conscience will be clear that you weren't the one who got me started."

Then he gave me his most winsome smile and put his arm around my waist. "How about some orange juice," he suggested.

"Orange juice coming up," I quickly agreed.

"We'll take grape juice!" the other three children chimed in. I rolled my eyes at their teasing.

1.
LIFE TEACHES THE DANGERS OF ALCOHOL.

We are foster parents, and many times the babies and small children who stay with us have parents who are more committed to their addictions than to the care of their children.

Our fourteen-year-old daughter Ashleigh, who loves these kids like a sister should and helps care for them, sees firsthand the devastating consequences of addiction.

2.

IF YOU'VE DONE DRUGS, OR ANYTHING ELSE, ADMIT IT TO YOUR CHILDREN.

Kids don't always stay away from liquor and drugs because of warnings from parents, teachers, and youth pastors. If you've used them yourself, though, and if you're comfortable doing so, share your bad experiences—your real-life testimony—with your children. It might keep them from ever getting started, or it may help them to stop. They can say, "Dad was right; dope is for dopes."

3.

BE PREPARED TO BE TESTED.

Amy has tested us several times to determine the depth of our unconditional love for her. The most recent episode involved smoking. She seemed to delight in letting us know she was doing it. The look on her face said, *So, what are you going to do about it?*

We didn't have to tell her how we felt about the habit. From the time she was a young girl, we had shared with her how we hoped she wouldn't partake of drugs and alcohol.

"We will not stop loving you, Amy, just because you smoke," we assured her, "but we won't allow it in the house. If you must smoke, go out on the porch."

She finally gave up this unhealthy habit.

4.
EXPLAIN THAT HIS BODY IS THE TEMPLE OF GOD AND SHOULDN'T BE DESECRATED WITH ABUSIVE SUBSTANCES.

Teenagers aren't dumb. They see what other kids their age do to their bodies by pumping them with alcohol, tobacco, or drugs. Since Chad respects the church and reads his Bible every day, we pointed him to 1 Corinthians 3:16,17: "Do you not know that you are the temple of God and that the Spirit of God dwells in you? If anyone defiles the temple of God, God will destroy him. For the temple of God is holy, which temple you are."

These verses had a profound effect on Chad. He wants to keep his body pure for the Lord.

5.
ASK YOUR KIDS WHO HAS BENEFITED FROM DRUGS.

On an outing at the beach, I asked my teenage son and daughter to name some famous people who have taken drugs and tell how such addictions have affected their lives. The list was long in no time: movie stars, singers, dancers, politicians, sports celebrities—all who had fallen from the graces of the community and their professions because of their drug use.

"Dad, I can't think of one person whose life was made better by taking drugs," Jory declared. He and his sister learned an important commonsense lesson that day.

6.
IF YOU WAIT UNTIL THEY'RE TEENAGERS TO TELL THEM THE DANGERS OF DRINKING, IT'S TOO LATE.

Today kids learn from an early age about drinking. They see it on television, hear about it from their friends, and are exposed to provocative and enticing advertisements. If you wait until they're teenagers, it's too late to get your message across. Start young.

7.
Can You Eliminate Your Child's Exposure to Drugs?

No, of course not, but I think there's a lot less exposure because we homeschool our children. In the public schools, there is greater peer pressure to use harmful substances.

8.
Give Me Five Good Reasons for Taking Drugs

Teenagers have more common sense than we as parents want to admit. Instead of harping on them day after day, "Don't ever take drugs," sit down with them and give them this challenge: "Tell me five good reasons for taking drugs, and I won't say a word against your doing so, if you choose to."

Cindy and Marla gazed at me for a minute. "It feels good," Cindy finally declared.

"But it's dangerous to feel good like that," Marla countered. "When you come down, you still have to face life and the reason you probably took the drugs in the first place."

I just let them go on for about thirty minutes, barely saying a word, amazed at how much they understood about the consequences of taking drugs. My comments consisted of statistics and scary information, all of which they already knew.

After Cindy's initial declaration that drugs made you feel good, we talked about other ways to feel good that are safe and healthy.

At the end of our talk Marla said matter-of-factly, "It doesn't make any sense to take drugs, does it, Mom?"

9.
SCARE THEM WITH FAMILY STATISTICS.

My son started smoking at sixteen, probably because almost all of his friends did. He smoked one pack a week for two years. I didn't know about his habit until I found some cigarettes in a pair of pants I was going to wash. Naturally I confronted him about it, using my best lecturing voice: "You've lost three of your grandparents to cancer, and all of their siblings died of cancer. There is so much cancer in our family, smoking is not something you should be doing."

His response? "I don't care. It's my body, and I'll do what I want with it."

I wanted to get angry, to yell at his stupidity, to forbid him in no uncertain terms from even touching another cigarette, but I knew none of those responses would change his mind. So, I told him what my mother had told me many years before: "If you're going to smoke, there's nothing I can do to stop you, because you'll sneak behind my back and do it. I want to make it clear I do not approve, and it won't be done in my house. But if you're home and you feel you absolutely have to have a cigarette, you can go outside, and I won't criticize you."

Todd never smoked at home and gave it up after two years, because it cost too much.

10.
There Comes a Time To Stop Bailing Them out of Trouble.

One night my son, while intoxicated, stole an unloaded gun from our house and went to a major hotel where his oldest brother was working. He got into a fight with a bouncer, and when it was discovered he had a gun, even unloaded, he was taken to jail. He'd been in jail several times before for drinking and driving, and several times we'd taken the car keys away from him.

Unlike previous times, though, when we'd bailed him out of jail, we turned our son over to God. Completely. When Jeff called from jail the following morning expecting us to bail him out, we refused.

This turned out to be the best thing we ever did for him, even though he was furious. When he finally got out of jail, with a friend's help, he came home, packed his clothes, and left.

About six months went by before he came home again, this time with a lovely young woman. After telling us of their plans to get married, Jeff cleared his throat and went on. "While in that dirty jail cell, I called upon God and asked Him to help me turn my life around, and He's answered my prayers."

The next week Jeff drove with his father to the store. The cab of the truck was silent except for the radio playing softly. My son broke the quiet with an unexpected question: "Dad, can you ever forgive me for the pain I've put you through?"

My husband smiled and put his arm around Jeff. "I already have," he said.

I thank the Lord for bringing my wandering son home. And I thank my husband for having a forgiving spirit and welcoming Jeff home with compassion, just as the father of the biblical prodigal son did.

11.
BE HONEST ABOUT DANGERS OF ALCOHOL.

Even though our immediate family is Christian and no alcohol is allowed in our home, I have a few relatives who battle alcoholism. I've talked with my sons candidly, explaining the dangers of drinking and exactly what happens to the mind and body when even one drink is consumed. I haven't handled it so much from a spiritual standpoint as from a common-sense way. I've told them that even before I became a Christian I had decided I would not drink, because I didn't want to find myself in the same stranglehold as some cousins of mine who continue their battle with alcohol.

Todd and Jordan appreciated that I treated them as

mature enough to understand the consequences of drinking. I didn't just say, "You aren't allowed to drink. Period."

12.
HONESTY MAY HURT,
BUT YOUR CHILDREN WILL BENEFIT.

It is difficult, as a baby boomer, to preach to my daughters not to use drugs. I feel like a hypocrite delivering such lectures because I not only experimented with drugs, I actually indulged in them for awhile. Thank goodness I can point to the time when I found a much better way to bring satisfaction into my life—a relationship with Jesus Christ. "Yes," I admit to my daughters, "I used drugs, but it wasn't smart. Being a Christian *is* smart, and your brain won't get fried along the way."

13.
BE AN EXAMPLE.

It's pretty hard to warn your kids about the dangers of drinking when you're drinking yourself. "But we're responsible drinkers" is the argument I hear from other parents. "Responsible until something happens you can't control, and then alcohol is a convenient place to turn to, to take away the pain," I answer back. How many responsible drinkers have never been drunk?

14.
FACE IT: MOST KIDS WILL EXPERIMENT.

Think ahead of time what your reaction will be if your child says he's on drugs or alcohol. What you don't want to do is get hysterical and say the wrong thing. Plan your response to deal most effectively with the situation.

15.
IT'S SCARY,
BUT LET THEM MAKE UP THEIR OWN MINDS.

We have always taught our children to be responsible for their own actions and the paths of their lives. Thus, I wanted them to explore the available information and make an informed decision concerning drugs. "Don't take it from me," I said. "Let the facts speak for themselves."

Both of my teenagers are dead set against the use of drugs and can proudly follow that determination because it is truly theirs. It is easier to defend your own position than defend the mandate of another.

16.
HAVE YOUR TEEN SMOKE IN FRONT OF YOU.

We were shocked to learn our seventeen-year-old daughter was smoking. My husband and I talked together about what to say to her to get her to quit. What we decided was to have Emily smoke in front of us. "We want to see you do it," we said.

So she did, starting with a bravado shrug of the shoulders. As she smoked, we said nothing, but merely looked at her. Two months later, when she'd given it up, she told us, "I couldn't stand the look of concern and disappointment in your eyes. If you had yelled at me, I would have been stubborn enough to keep it up. But those looks haunted me and broke my heart."

17.
DON'T PRETEND YOU'VE NEVER DONE DRUGS BEFORE.

I smoked marijuana for awhile when the father of my two children and I were separated. The kids saw what it did to me. I wasn't going to church at the time and felt my life was falling apart. I was a terrible example for them. However, once I renewed my commitment to the Lord, and my husband and I got back together again, I talked with my kids openly about my drug use. "I've been there. I've done drugs. If you have any questions, please ask me first. I can save you a lot of grief."

They have, and neither my son nor daughter has done drugs to this day.

18.
IT CAN HAPPEN TO YOU.

Talking about their drinking exploits used to be a favorite pastime of certain kids at my daughter's high school. But that was before one of their friends became drunk and crashed his Jeep. He'd come to a T in the road and hadn't stopped. There were no skid marks. He cleared a ditch, hit the side of a tree, and then slammed into a traffic sign and knocked it fifty feet into the woods. The paramedics pulled him out from under the front tire of his vehicle. He had to have plastic surgery, because his face was so mangled.

His friends at school cried and talked about the accident the whole week before spring break. Someone said he'd been pressured to drink or smoke something at a party that night. Many of the kids vowed not to drink anymore because of what happened. He was really important to his friends, because he thought of others above himself. One girl said, "I think that God let him live to remind us not to drink and drive. In fact, not to drink at all."

19.
"IF YOU EVER DO DRUGS..."

I told my boys, "It's against the law; it's a sin; it'll mess you up big time, and if you *ever* do drugs, I'll dump you at the police station so fast, it'll make your head swim!"

Triumph here, so far.

20.
A GOOD DETERRENT IS TO LET YOUR CHILD SEE SOMEONE WHO IS DRUNK.

My teenage daughter and I work at the same company. At the annual company Christmas party this past year, another teenage worker, whom my daughter knows, came to the party drunk. On the way, she had had a minor accident with her car and wanted Sharon and me to lie to her parents about it. Her obnoxious behavior during the party made a powerful impression on Sharon who has, in the past, wondered if being drunk really makes people act differently. Now she knows.

BATTLE OF WILLS

For He. . .appointed a law in Israel, which He commanded our fathers, that they should make them known to their children; that they may set their hope in God, and not forget the works of God, but keep His commandments; and may not be like their fathers, a stubborn and rebellious generation, a generation that did not set its heart aright, and whose spirit was not faithful to God.

PSALM 78:5,7,8

"It's going to be the neatest weekend, Mom," Lisa gushed the minute she got home from school and found me in the kitchen cooking her favorite meal, Seafood Delight. "Just six of us girls, all my best friends, at this cabin up in Big Bear. We're leaving Friday right after school—"

I dropped a can of tuna fish in the baking dish, and milk splattered over the edge and onto the counter. "Whoa, Girl. Slow down. This is the first I've heard of these plans."

Lisa gave me an enthusiastic kiss, the kind I get when she wants me to become wonderful-mother-who'll-let-her-do-exactly-what-she-wants-to-do. "It's Jennifer's parents' cabin, Mom. You've heard me talk about it."

"Yes-s-s-s."

"Well, a bunch of us are going up there this weekend."

"With what adults?" I mopped up the spilled milk with a paper towel.

"Uh. . .no adults exactly, but Jennifer's sister is going. She's almost out of college and is very dependable."

"For what?"

"Mom, she's mature. She won't let us get into trouble."

"I don't know that."

"I'll have Jennifer's mom call you."

I looked at my adorable, redheaded daughter. "I'm sorry, Lisa, but if there won't be at least two adults there who I can talk to first and know I can trust, I can't let you go." I then received Lisa's most-terrible-mother-in-the-whole-world-who-doesn't-ever-understand-her-teenage-daughter look. Oh well, that's the price one pays for the privilege of motherhood.

Lisa only ate one forkful of Seafood Delight at dinner. That told me I was in her major doghouse. There were long sighs over dessert which she didn't eat at all.

Her three brothers groaned with each one and told her to get over it. She looked at them, at me, and then at her father, her eyes full of despair. She went to bed at eight-thirty and didn't even play her favorite CDs.

On Sunday evening she received a call from Jennifer that lasted an hour. She didn't tell me about it.

On Monday, after school, she came home in a happy mood, smiling, and gave me a kiss on the cheek, one of those long ones that told me I was back in her favor.

"Why are you so chipper?" I asked her.

"I just learned I have the smartest mother."

I dropped the load of clothes I was carrying to the washing machine and stared at her. "You have the what?"

"A smart mother."

"What have I done?"

She came close to me. "Mom, guess what? The girls who went to the mountain got stopped by the police for speeding and causing an accident. Some little old lady—"

"Probably in her forties," I embellished.

"How'd you know? Anyway, Jennifer's sister was driving her folks' car and ran into this lady's car. Did two thousand dollars worth of damage. Jennifer's parents are furious about that and about the big ticket Monica received. She has to go to court because the lady says she received whiplash and is suing her. The police found beer in the car. All the girls are in major trouble. Can you believe that? I'm so glad I wasn't there."

I plopped my hands on my hips. "But you would have been if you'd talked me into it. Remember how we battled over it?"

"Sure, Mom, but I knew you wouldn't let me go."

"Then why did you fight me so much?"

"Because I wanted to go. . .but I didn't want to go. I knew I could count on you to make up my mind for me."

I gathered up the clothes and tossed them into her arms. "Help me with the laundry. Maybe there are other things I can change your mind about."

1.
WHERE'S THE MANUAL.

Sixteen-year-old Brandon has let me know just how unhappy he is over some of the ways I resolve our differences. I tell him, "You didn't come with an instruction manual. I'm doing the best I can."

2.
TALK TO THEM.

"Talk to me and ask me how I feel about things," fifteen-year-old Sam begged, even pointing his finger at us. "The reason I fight you so much about doing things is that you never ask how I feel. All you do is give orders, orders, orders."

3.

CHOOSE YOUR BATTLES.

Don't sweat the small stuff. Don't make every decision a major battle. Does it really matter if the colors of your daughter's outfit don't match? Yes, you want to teach her about style, but maybe she's not ready to be taught.

It's okay to let children have their way if it's not a life-threatening or spiritually threatening situation, if you only have to bend a little, within the limits of your parenting conscience.

When kids make their own decisions, their self-confidence increases. They also learn a powerful lesson when they discover they've made a mistake. And maybe they'll come to realize you're pretty good at making the right decisions after all.

4.

HUMBLE PIE DOESN'T TASTE GOOD, BUT EAT IT IF YOU MUST.

More than once, I'm sorry to say, I've lost my temper in an argument with my daughter. More than once, I've said unkind, unfair, or even untrue things. More than once, I've had to apologize for not believing her, trusting her, and jumping to conclusions. More than once, I've been glad she has it in her heart to forgive a dad who's not perfect.

5.
TIME-OUTS WORK.

We are going through a tough time with fifteen-year-old Greg. "You don't understand anything I'm saying to you," he rants at us. Of course, we think the problem lies with him. If we say yes, he says no. If we say it's sunny, he says, "Can't you see the dark clouds?"

In our adult Sunday school class, we have discussed how to discipline teenagers. One mother said, "Time-outs work well for our daughter." I found that hard to believe since we'd stopped using time-outs for Greg when he was ten years old. But the next time he became argumentative and angry to the point of raising his voice—he wanted to stay out later than his curfew—I told him to take a time-out. At first he just stared at me like I was crazy, but then he stomped off to his room.

He stayed in there for fifteen minutes, playing his CDs loudly. Loudly! I was about to tear my hair out from the noise when it suddenly stopped. Greg came out of his room and said, calmly, "I'll be home by eleven, Dad."

Don't ask me why the time-out concept worked; it just did. Perhaps being given time to think about the situation without the pressure of my insistence caused Greg's behavior change.

6.
GIVE THEM DISTANCE.

When my daughter decided to move out on her eighteenth birthday, I knew I had to let her distance herself from me. Although her decision hurt me terribly, I let her know I loved her and that I wouldn't force my will on her. I prayed constantly, because I really didn't have control over the situation, and I kept the lines of communication open.

It took approximately a year for her to see things in a different light, and now our mother-daughter relationship is stronger than ever. I had to let go and pray to God to bring good people into her life while she was pushing me away. I also let Him know He was totally in charge, and since I trusted Him, I knew that in the end, somehow, things would be all right.

7.
LET THEM MAKE THEIR OWN MISTAKES —
OVER SMALL MATTERS.

Today's teenagers think they're pretty smart and mature. They don't want to be hassled over every little decision, and, as they grow older, they want to make more and more of their own decisions. That means they'll make mistakes. But they know that.

My fourteen-year-old daughter has said to me, "You shouldn't say, 'Don't do this because I did it when I was a kid, and it was bad for me.' If I make my own mistakes, it will stick with me longer. Now, the really bad things like taking drugs and drinking, yeah, you need to keep telling me. I'm grateful for warnings about bad stuff. But little things, like breaking curfew, or not studying for a test, I need to learn the consequences myself."

8.
BEWARE OF COMPARING SITUATIONS.

Tara wanted to get her ears pierced. I said, "Remember your friend, Gretchen, how her ears got infected?" Tara surprised me by saying, "Well, I'm not Gretchen, and I'll be more careful. You know, Mom, when I want to do something and I tell you that someone else's mom has let her do that, you say, 'I'm not her mom, I'm your mother, so don't compare.' But you're comparing me to Gretchen."

I saw her point.

9.
PLAN YOUR CONFRONTATION.

If you're a business person, you wouldn't walk into an important meeting without your thoughts in order and some objectives that you want to accomplish. If you're about to have a "meeting" with your child over his behavior, likewise you should write down your thoughts and objectives before confronting him. In short, you should have some idea how to resolve the conflict. Besides, in the heat of battle you could forget your most important points if they're not written down. Since there is no more important business than raising your child, be prepared for that meeting when you both will share your feelings and goals.

10.
WE ARE WHO WE ARE.

When battling your child over an important issue, remind yourself that you have your basic personality, and your child has hers. To expect her to become you, to be your clone, is unrealistic. However, also remember that *you* are the grown-up with more life experience. Use those life skills to work within your child's personality.

11.
THERE'S ONLY ONE PLACE TO TURN — JESUS.

Jennifer was known in high school for her Christian faith and was affectionately nicknamed "Air Jehovah" by some. In a large school where sex, drugs, and violence were the norm, Jesus was reflected in Jennifer's life.

Kids came to her whenever they needed a safe harbor and a steady boat.

Jennifer set sail for college. Things did not remain as they were. We now fight a battle of the wills. . .and keep seeking the Lord to mend our hearts and hers. Jennifer, these days, smells of smoke, has bloodshot eyes, and finds no reason to call home. The family suffers as she tries to grow up.

All the strong parenting we did has not worked. There is only one place to turn, and that is to Jesus. My husband and I pray each morning for guidance.

Jennifer has now moved out of our home to live with a girlfriend. We agreed to let her go, assuring her that we loved her and that she could always come back home. But we also reminded her that her moral standards no longer lined up with our Christian home and that we were still rearing two other teens. "We will always love you, Jennifer, as will Jesus," were our last words to her.

We do not know what will come of this. It is hard to wait and to grieve over your child. Every day, aloud, Jennifer's father and I lift her name to the Lord. We know He hears. We expectantly wait.

12.
BE IN CHARGE.

Don't be rushed into a decision. Use a firm, gentle, matter-of-fact voice when you tell your children your answer. When they detect resolve in your voice, they'll be less likely to resist.

13.

Use the Same Strategy You'd Use with a Three Year Old.

Our fifteen-year-old son is a handful. Our three-year-old granddaughter, who stays with us during the day, is a handful. Because the way they behave is amazingly similar at times, I find that the discipline I give little Kari also works for big Jared.

14.

Are You Suffocating Your Child?

My son's best friend has explained to me why kids rebel again their parents. "It's because you don't let go of us. We feel suffocated."

"But we love you and want to protect you," I countered.

"That doesn't work," he said. "It makes us feel like we're caged in, and we're too big for the cage."

15.
CALM DOWN AND TALK.

Here's the quickest way to incur my son's anger: be angry myself when I confront him over a problem. I raise my voice; he raises his voice. Sometimes we end up shouting at each other, and later I'm ashamed.

"Just talk to me," Steve says. "Talk out your anger. You're the parent. Help me talk out mine, too."

When did he get so smart?

16.
IT'S HARD TO BE A MOM AND A PAL.

"But Suzie's mom is so co-o-ol," fourteen-year-old Chelsy exclaimed. "She has a tattoo on her stomach and lets Suzie skip school when she's tired, go out on dates on weeknights, and—"

"Sorry, Kiddo, I'm not Suzie's mom. I'm yours, and if I have to make you dislike me for a couple of hours—or years—to prove I love you, I will, because I'm not afraid of doing the right thing on your behalf."

I went through this same tug-of-war with Chelsy's older sister Blaine, who is now twenty-five. Today Blaine calls me her "bestest-best friend." Brownie points? Maybe, but how many young women plan a day a week to do stuff with their mothers. . .without the mom's prodding? Blaine does, and I hope Chelsy will, too.

17.
DON'T SPEAK TO THEM WHEN THEY'RE ANGRY.

When Sarah gets angry and tries to pick an argument, I refuse to get caught up in her emotions. I tell her I'll discuss the problem when she calms down. Then I go about my business as though she isn't there. I sing a song or start dusting the living room or preparing supper. I'm not saying we don't ever argue, but when I'm in control of myself, the situation is eased.

18.
BECAUSE I'M YOUR MOM,
AND I SAID SO.

When my daughters used to pressure me to let them do something I didn't feel right about, I felt I needed to explain myself. My husband wisely told me, "It's okay to answer, 'Because I'm your mother, and I said so.' They won't like it, but they'll accept it."

Now when I know in my heart a decision is right, I don't rush to justify it. My new attitude shows that this is what needs to be done. Period. There are no arguments or tugs-of-war for control of the situation. I honestly suspect that most of the time my daughters are happy I'm taking the decision away from them and putting it on my adult shoulders.

19.
SHOW THEM YOU LOVE THEM
BY SAYING NO.

After we had just moved into a new neighborhood, Jeanine, a freshman, wanted to go to a football game. There were two problems: The game was clear across the state, and Jeanine would be riding with a friend I didn't know well. They wouldn't get home until well after midnight. I didn't want her to go, so I said no. She said yes. I said no.

She took off up the street. We are about one long block from the main highway. As I followed her in the car, I rolled down the window and said, "Get in the car." She wouldn't. We got to the highway, and she started going south, and I followed her, repeating my command. This went on for another few blocks. Cars had to pass me.

Finally Jeanine got into the car after this fifteen-minute battle of wills. We drove home. She sat outside by the fire pit and wouldn't come in. I said nothing more but watched to make sure she didn't try to sneak off.

Years later she told me, "I knew that night that you really cared about me, Mom."

20.
There Has to be a Reason for Saying No.

Phillip knows when we say no, there's a reason for it, that we're not just saying the word arbitrarily. We may not always give him the reason, but if he asks, we will. Since he was very young, he could repeat our words in his sleep: "If we say no, there's a good reason for it."

21.
Give Them Permission to Complain.

When my daughter was thirteen, I consulted a wonderful Christian counselor about her argumentative attitude. The counselor explained a technique that works well with teenagers. "When you're going to tell your child something you know she will balk at, preface your comments with this sentence: 'I know you aren't going to like my decision, so I give you permission to yell and complain for ten minutes.' Teenagers rarely yell or complain when given permission to do so."

This technique works nine times out of ten. Anna just stares at me a moment, then turns and goes to her room. I notice she does shut her door a little harder than usual, though.

CHURCH AND FAITH IN ACTION

All your children shall be taught by the
LORD, and great shall be the peace of your
children.

ISAIAH 54:13

"I'm not going to church today," our son, Terry, announced one Sunday morning when it was time to leave for the services, and I questioned his grubby attire.

"I thought you enjoyed it," I said.

"Nope."

"But you've been faithful in going to the youth group on Wednesday nights."

"Waste of time."

"You said you had good friends there," I reminded him.

"Maybe not so good."

I looked at my watch. My husband and the other three kids were waiting in the car.

"It isn't because I didn't get your favorite black shirt washed, is it?"

"Noooo."

The phone rang. Terry sprang to answer it, no doubt hoping it was a call from the President who wanted his advice on national policy in Afghanistan.

"Hi, Jennifer. . .uh, sure. . .absolutely. . .see you then."

Terry plopped the phone back on the receiver and gave me his most winning smile.

"Give me five minutes, and I'll be ready." He dashed out of the kitchen and up the stairs toward his room, then he stopped at the top of the landing. "Are you sure you didn't wash my favorite black shirt?"

Once we were settled in the car, I asked casually, "Who was on the phone?" I glanced in the rearview mirror and saw Terry's smile broaden from ear to ear.

"Jennifer Hunnicut," he answered. "She wants me to sit by her in Sunday school today."

"I see."

The Lord works in mysterious ways, His wonders to perform, I thought to myself.

1.
TEACH YOUR CHILDREN SERVANT EVANGELISM.

When we wanted our teenage sons to demonstrate their Christian faith actively, we instituted a program of "servant evangelism." Our first experience was giving a car wash and not charging any money. Did we get puzzled looks!

Then we went to the park and handed out ice-cold drinks or fruit pops on hot, humid days.

We held a carnival in a housing project (featuring games, music, and hot dogs) just before school started for the year. We called such an activity "Matthew's Party" after the apostle who brought his friends to meet Jesus. It was easy to play with these children and tell them over and over how much Jesus loved them. The "prizes" were supplies that would prepare them for school.

On April 15 we went to the local post office and gave away cookies and coffee, free stamps and forms for last-minute income tax filers. Some stressed-out folks needed a party atmosphere that day.

Always, we heard the question, "Why are you doing this?" Our answer? "We are doing this as a community project to demonstrate the love of God in a practical way."

Our boys saw again and again how easy it is to communicate the love of God and share our faith.

2.
TRY "JEWISH SUNDAY SCHOOL."

Because we wanted to impart to our children a faith that was more than ideas and facts, we coined the phrase, "Jewish Sunday school," based on the verses from Deuteronomy 6:6,7: "And these words. . .shall be in your heart. You shall teach them diligently to your children, and shall talk of them when you sit in your house, when you walk by the way, when you lie down, and when you rise up."

Each moment should be an opportunity to speak about our faith. When we watch TV together, for instance, we talk during the commercials about acts of TV violence we've just seen (this can be on the network newscasts as well as on programs we thought would be appropriate to watch), adulterous situations, dishonesty, and foolish choices. These become teaching moments that inspire questions: "What would you feel if your wife kissed another man like that? What if you had a friend who lied to you like that?"

In one day, there are an incredible number of teaching moments.

3.
GOD KNOWS THE DESIRE OF YOUR HEART
TO SEE YOUR CHILDREN SAVED.

In raising my children, I've always held to two promises found in the Bible: (1) Acts 16:31: ". . .Believe on the Lord Jesus Christ, and you will be saved, you and your household"; (2) Acts 2:38,39: "Then Peter said to them, 'Repent, and let every one of you be baptized in the name of Jesus Christ for the remission of sins; and you shall receive the gift of the Holy Spirit. For the promise is to you and to your children.' "

Now that my son and daughter are in their teens, God has given them wonderful youth leaders. My son wants to go into the ministry as a missionary.

4.
WHO'S GOING TO MODEL
WHAT A WIFE AND MOTHER SHOULD BE,
IF NOT YOU?

Girls need models of godly mothers and wives. Automatically, they'll look at the relationship between Mom and Dad and judge whether it reflects Christ and the church. The church gives respect, honor, and praise to Christ, and Christ gives love, honor, and protection to the church. Girls need to see Mom under Dad's umbrella of protection, a hierarchy set up by God. Girls also need to see Dad treating Mom in a gentle, Christlike manner, showing unconditional love and looking to no other.

5.
MEMORIZE SCRIPTURE WITH YOUR KIDS.

My wife and I memorize Bible passages with our three children. We review these daily and then ask questions that cause our teens to dig deeper for the answers. "Thanks, Dad," are my favorite words to hear when my children understand an important scriptural truth.

6.
DAD NEEDS TO BE AN EXAMPLE.

There's nothing that lets a teenager know he's loved more than hearing his father pray for him. Usually this is done at the supper table. To have a father who openly asks for God's help, regularly, is a tremendous testimony to a youngster.

7.
LET YOUR CHILDREN SEE HOW IMPORTANT THE BIBLE IS TO YOU.

Because we want our children to know how much we respect and adhere to the teachings of the Bible, we read and study daily and then discuss passages with them. We're not trying to show off our Christianity to Megan and David by letting them see us reading our Bibles. We just want them to know that the Bible is the most important book in our home.

8.
BE SURE THEY KNOW THE BASICS.

While training up your child in the way he should go, stress the basics of your faith more than the rituals particular to your church. What are the crucial truths you want your child never to forget in his walk with God? Is it prayer? Reading the Bible? Listening to God speak day by day?

The structure of your church worship may not always be available to your child, or he may not be interested in participating that way when he is older.

Life is about change. For me, peace of mind is knowing that my son, David, knows how to communicate with God in the most basic of ways, no matter where he is or in what circumstances. Make faith simple.

9.
THE BUCK STOPS
WITH THE BIBLE

In our home, the Bible is where the buck stops because only the Bible has the answers to all life's questions. Teens need to be taught how to use God's Word specifically (if they didn't already learn when they were younger). To illustrate, I open the Bible, showing them the crease in the middle, and then I point from all directions to the crease. All of life needs to be viewed through what this book says because it is *truth*. Teens can feel comfortable because the Bible provides their "walls" of guidance.

10.
TEACH GOD'S SOVEREIGNTY.

If the sovereignty of God is taught properly, and you use the Word's authority in your parenting experiences, the kids won't argue with you, because they know they can't argue with God.

11.
TEENS NEED PROOF
ABOUT GOD'S VALIDITY

The truth of God's Word can be demonstrated to teenagers by showing how the prophecies from the Old and New Testaments have proven true, over and over. This is an exciting family Bible topic that we discuss once a week around the dinner table. I explain to John and Jimmy that, long after all things pass away, the Word will remain (John 1), because it is Christ in the flesh, and it will judge the world. That means us.

12.
TEACH YOUR CHILDREN ABOUT GOD
ANY WAY YOU CAN.

When I married again, to a man I thought was a Christian and who had been raised in a denomination I respected, I was shocked to learn his real philosophy. He believed that everything and everyone is made of God, so we all become as God when we die, and that everyone will go to heaven because God won't send anyone to hell.

We went to a new church together for the first six months of our marriage, but then he became jealous of my involvement with the church and told me I should spend all my time with him and not with a bunch of do-gooders. He has verbally bullied me to the point where I've decided to go along with him for awhile, to see if an acquiescent spirit will change his mind, and he'll agree to go to church with me again.

While he doesn't care if my two sons go to church, in the home we do not talk about God. Whenever I am with my sons alone, however, I share with them what I've learned in the Bible, and we pray together. I know my Christian example is limited, but it's all I can do for the moment. Joe and Peter enjoy being with their friends and involved in the activities at the church. I have to trust the Lord to inspire others to reach out to them at this time with the message of how to live a Christ-centered life.

13.
REMAIN TRUE TO YOUR
"PLUMB LINE" (AMOS 7:7)

Parents should remain true to their "plumb lines," in other words, their code of Christian ethics and morals but at the same time, not become Pharisees. I always strive to be "Jesus with skin on." To be a Christian in our most precious relationships is what Christ calls us to do, and our relationships with our children are vital.

14.
WHEN WE DON'T KNOW WHAT TO DO. . .WHAT THEN?

Our nineteen-year-old son, who is away at college, is communicating over the Internet with a woman who is twenty-eight years old. To us, her contacts with him have been very suspicious, and now he's planning to meet her in another state to talk with her face-to-face.

We've warned him she may be up to no good, but he assures us she's a warm and caring person. We've run out of talk. All we can do now is put the situation in the hands of the Lord, palms down, which means we can't grab it back again, not if we really trust Him to guide us through this valley.

Palms-down faith is tough.

15.
TEACH TEENS THE WAY BACK.

Child rearing is the most difficult task anyone can undertake, but it is also the most rewarding experience life can offer. I am happy to say that I have "good children"—yes, they have their trials, some pretty serious, but they know their way back.

They have been taught the principles and truths needed to repent and progress on the correct path, and they've had to use courage more than once to take the steps necessary to come back—to us and to the Lord.

16.
ATTEND A CHURCH THAT SUPPORTS THE FAMILY.

I belong to a church that supports and teaches the importance of the family unit. Once a month, for the twenty-eight years I have been married, I have attended a class that teaches how to raise families. I have even taught a few. Our church produces wonderful manuals that cover most parenting subjects and how to teach them.

17.
TEACHING FAITH IS A DECISION.

When my wife and I married, we decided that teaching Christ would be foremost in the development of our children. Knowing that God has given humankind the right to choose, and that we could not "force" our children to accept Him, we, nonetheless, did all we could to present the gospel to them. We used the Scriptures daily to teach, to answer questions (on not just religious issues but real-life dilemmas), to reinforce our standards, and to show our love of God.

Because faith is something that can only be taught by example, we attended church, participated in service projects, worked in the church, and prayed over meals, at bedtime, and over everything else. We knew our children were watching what we were doing. By putting our faith foremost in their minds, the choices that could have drawn them into the evils of the world were more evident and became more distasteful. Eventually they chose as we did—to serve God. How we thank Him!

18.
TAKE A STAND AGAINST IMMORAL LYRICS.

When I really listened to the lyrics of the music coming from my son's room, I was shocked. In my day, using such language would have resulted in having one's mouth washed out with soap. I walked right into his room and asked Tyler what he was playing. He showed me a tape his friend had given him, but even as he gave it to me to see, guilt rushed over his face. "I like the music," he said weakly.

"But the words are not those we should be listening to," I told him gently, aware of his consternation.

"I'll give it back to Jerry," he promised. I was glad I had not flown into a tirade, threatening to ground him for bringing that "trash" into our house. Kids need guidance, not derision.

19.
LOOK TO THE FAITH OF A CHILD.

Our family watched a wonderful television movie about the Lochness monster. A little girl swore she had seen the monster. A man didn't believe her. "I have to see it before I can believe it," he told her. "No," she answered, "you've got to believe it before you can see it."

Isn't that also true about faith?

20.
MAKE CHURCH AND FAITH NUMBER ONE
IN YOUR HOME.

Because our faith has always been our number-one priority, we believe in going to church faithfully. Our son and daughter have been raised to understand that all their lives, and they know there is no excuse for missing church, other than sickness.

When they've tried to break free from that habit, and they have, here's what we say: "This is what our family does. When you move out and support yourself and have your own life, you may do what you choose."

We have a plaque by the front door that quotes those famous words of Joshua (Joshua 24:15): "But as for me and my house, we will serve the LORD."

Adult friends who have been lax in displaying Christian faith in the home and in attending church now find themselves fighting with their teenagers. Besides battling to stay home from church, their children are fighting for the right to do truly questionable things.

Habits are hard to break. We've made our faith and church attendance a habit we don't ever want to break.

21.
FATHERS NEED TO SET AN EXAMPLE FOR THEIR CHILDREN.

When my kids were growing up, I wasn't a church attender, but my wife was, and a faithful one. She took the kids with her every Sunday and also during the week to various activities. When Skip got to be a teenager, he rebelled and didn't want to go anymore. He fought to stay home with me, and I let him. We did fun things together on Sundays. My wife felt bad about this, and I knew it, but I was flattered that my son was choosing me over church—and God, if I can be honest enough to say that.

Today my son is a mess. He's into drugs and is living with a woman who is not his wife. They have two illegitimate children. My heart breaks to think I might have kept this from happening if I'd been the kind of father who supported my son's early faith and church attendance. Yes, I know he made his own choices, but I was a role model, and a faulty one for him.

22.
CHURCH PROVIDES A STEADY INFLUENCE.

When my daughter started ninth grade, she didn't want to go to church anymore. She had new friends who thought it was a sissy thing to do. While I gave her all the standard reasons why she should be there, I didn't want to force her to go. How many people have you heard say, "My parents forced me to go to church, and I ended up hating it"? I didn't want that to happen to Casey. So I gave her the choice of attending or not attending, hoping she'd learn a valuable lesson.

It didn't work that way. She chose not to go to church, and at the same time chose to run around with kids her mother and I didn't approve of. By the end of ninth grade, she was a wild kid I hardly recognized. That's when I put my foot down. "From now on," I told her one day, "you don't go out with anyone during the week unless you've gone to church on Sunday."

Was I in the doghouse! But what she was turning into scared me into taking a strong stand. That's when I began to pray that God would change her life. "I'll get her to church, Lord. You speak to her heart." I knew the church would be the positive influence that could keep Casey steady in an unsteady world.

The partnership worked. After about a year, Casey became a believer and since then has helped other teenagers who think they want to give up the things of God for the things of the world.

23.
PRAY YOUR CHILD HAS A RELATIONSHIP WITH GOD.

A parent's job is so much easier if the child has a personal relationship with God. That way, the child isn't going to church because you, the parent, say he should. There's nothing a kid hates more than to be told over and over what to do. After countless reminders, the child will turn against you. Church attendance by itself is meaningless; personal salvation is the goal every parent should have for his child.

24.
DON'T MAKE YOUR CHILD FEEL GUILTY FOR HER DOUBTS.

When I was a teenager, even though I attended church all the time, I had doubts about God's existence and the truth of the Bible. But I was never comfortable letting my parents know how I felt, and it took far too many years for my understanding to mature, years I wasted in not serving the Lord.

I've talked with my two teenage daughters and let them know it's normal to doubt. Even one of Jesus' disciples, Thomas, openly expressed his doubt, and probably the others shared some degree of confusion themselves. After all, faith deals with the unknown.

"I know you think I'm too old (I'm thirty-seven) to understand what you're going through in your Christian walk," I told Susy and Tristan, "but I remember perfectly what I felt as a teenager—all the questions and insecurities. I want you to know I'm here for you, ready to talk about anything spiritual that troubles you."

25.
UNCONDITIONAL LOVE
V.
UNCONDITIONAL APPROVAL.

We have told our children that, while we love them with an unconditional love, meaning we will always love them, that does not mean we will give them our unconditional approval no matter what they do. There is a difference.

26.
REMEMBER THE GOLDEN RULE.

At the beginning of the fall, I brought a plaque from home to show my ninth-grade Sunday school class, a class that includes my daughter. Written on this plaque, which hangs over the front door of our house, is a verse from Jesus' Sermon on the Mount (Matthew 7:12): "Therefore, whatever you want men to do to you, do also to them, for this is the Law and the Prophets." The world calls this the Golden Rule.

The only homework assignment I give my students all year is to come back to class the next week and tell me something, anything, they've done to show they understood what that phrase means.

Whenever I see one of those kids—in church, at the mall, in the grocery store—they'll say, "Hey, Mrs. Wallace, listen to this. . . ." and they'll proceed to tell me a Golden Rule story. They're learning to practice good faith.

27.
LIVE LIKE JESUS.

The main rule at our house is "Live like Jesus." What else do we need to teach our children? Jesus wouldn't do drugs. He wouldn't get drunk or drive while under the influence. He wouldn't have sex before marriage. He wouldn't swear or allow himself to tell or listen to dirty jokes. He wouldn't steal or lie or cheat on His homework.

28.
WHAT WOULD JESUS THINK OF THAT BEHAVIOR?

At the supper table, my children often share what their classmates did in school that wasn't good, or how their friends misbehave and lie to their parents. My wife and I put in our two cents and ask the kids to say what Jesus would think of that behavior. Good or bad? Acceptable or not?

Being a parent isn't rocket science. It's easy, provided Mom and Dad live by the same rules they set down for their kids. Of course, our lives have to be genuine because kids can spot a phony with their eyes shut. If parents don't really believe in the power of God to transform lives and guide daily living, the youngsters could adopt this attitude, too. If Dad sneaks a drink or if Mom reads a racy book, while telling the children not to do the same, trouble looms on the horizon. Parents, like their children, need to ask of themselves, "What would Jesus think of that behavior?"

DATING

So Jacob served seven years for Rachel, and they seemed only a few days to him because of the love he had for her.

GENESIS 29:20

"Mom, I'm in big trouble," my fifteen-year-old son, David, said to me.

I wish I had a ten-dollar bill for every time I heard those words.

"Tell me about it," I said to him.

David sat down at the kitchen table, and I got us two bowls of carrot sticks to munch on. (Okay, okay, it was two bowls of chocolate chip mint ice cream.)

"There's this girl, Janey Robertson," David began.

"Okay."

"I know her from school. She comes to the basketball games and likes the way I play."

"Yes."

"You know I'm tall for my age, and mature."

"I've noticed that."

"She likes my sense of humor."

"So do I."

"Today, Janey asked me to take her to a humongous picnic at her church. It's run by the teenagers. She's some kind of officer in the group." He waited for me to collapse from understanding. I didn't.

"So?" I said.

"Janey is a senior. She's the homecoming queen. Guys go bonkers over her."

"And?"

"I'm a freshman and. . .*I don't drive.*"

"Ah."

"Mom, senior girls go out with college guys, not high school freshmen."

"I see. She doesn't know you're only fifteen?"

"No. How can I tell her I don't drive?"

"Not to mention that you don't even date yet."

"Mom, you know that up until now I've just liked being with a group of kids rather than one girl. But Janey. . ."

"Is different?"

"Yeah."

I put down my spoon and leaned across the table. "You do it like this, David: 'Janey, I'd love to go to the church picnic with you. What time shall I meet you there?'"

He paused to think it over. "No good. She specifically asked me to pick her up."

I sighed. "Okay, try this: 'Janey, I'd love to go to the church picnic with you, but I can't pick you up because I don't drive.'"

"Tell her the truth?"

I sat back. "A novel concept, I admit, but most of the time it works best."

"I don't know. . . ."

"Can't she drive? After all, she asked you to the picnic, and this is the age of equality."

David's eyes brightened. "Mom, you're a genius."

"Well. . ." I shrugged my shoulders in humble admission of a truth he should have known from day one. Will they never learn? I treated myself to another well-deserved spoonful of chocolate chip mint ice cream.

1.

AS AN INTRODUCTION TO DATING, LET THEM GO OUT FIRST IN ODD-NUMBERED GROUPS.

Group interaction is a good introduction to dating. When Rachel entered her freshman year in high school, many of her friends automatically assumed they had the green light to date. While my husband and I didn't think Rachel was ready at age fifteen to become part of a "couple," at the same time we didn't want to squash her social development. Our solution? She could go out in mixed groups on weekends, provided the group was an odd number. That meant that while there were some boys and girls paired off, the group as a whole was meant to stay that way—as a group! The pressure was off Rachel to act like she was on a date, and she could just get to know guys as guys and not necessarily as love interests.

2.
You, Not Your Friends, Decide When Your Child Is Ready for Dating.

Don't push teens into dating or boy-girl situations if they're not ready, and that means even if your closest friends' children can't stop making plans. Our painfully shy son is a sophomore in high school and, while he certainly is aware when a gorgeous girl enters the room, he's not ready to submit himself to school dances or other potentially painful social situations. He enjoys sports and hanging with his friends, so, as parents, we say let God take care of the rest.

3.
Teach Your Child to Date Responsibly.

Our son Jason was asked to the senior prom by a girl in his class he didn't really like. She had neither an amiable disposition nor good standing with her peers and the school faculty. "What should I do?" Jason asked us. Together we confronted the issue of her reputation and the fact that she was, personality-wise, his complete opposite.

"Why not ask a girl you'll feel comfortable with and decline Amanda's offer?" I suggested.

"I don't know if I can do that, Dad," Jason said. "I wouldn't know what to say, and I don't want to hurt her feelings."

After we commended his concern for her feelings, I added, "Better a few moments of awkwardness than an entire evening of insincere pleasantries. The decision is yours, of course."

Jason finally decided to decline her offer and asked a girl he really liked. Needless to say, he had a great time.

4.
DATING IS PRACTICING FOR DIVORCE.

We told Maryssa she could not "date" until she was sixteen. (That's what our parents told us!) But what is dating? My husband figured out that dating is just practicing for divorce because by dating different people, Maryssa will have a series of broken relationships. Now we encourage her to have friends. Telling a boy, "Let's just be friends," doesn't have to be negative. In fact, the best kind of love should grow out of a good friendship.

Good friendships can become the training ground for learning mutual trust and unselfishness prior to marriage. We say, "Every date is a potential mate. How serious do you want to get with this person?"

5.
HOW TO SAY NO TO DANCES.

Ashley was invited to a school dance by a boy she particularly liked. When her mother and I said no, she got upset with us and asked that familiar question every parent of a teenager hears a dozen times a week: "Why?"

We showed her 1 Corinthians 7:1: "It is good for a man not to touch a woman."

"This is talking about sexual arousal between unmarried people," we told Ashley honestly. "That is not a good thing according to God's Word. When couples dance, men touch women. Such a situation can lead to too much intimacy, and that's why we don't want you going to dances."

"But boys touch me at church," Ashley countered. "I mean, they shake my hand, or jokingly punch me on the arm."

"That's different," I told her. "Those aren't intimate touches."

When the familiar pout of her lower lip began, I quickly suggested, "On the night of the dance, let's invite your favorite family over for games."

She brightened. "Or could I have a slumber party with some girlfriends?"

"Sure."

Her accepting smile reassured us tremendously. After all, we acted as we did because we care for her well-being and want to be obedient to God's Word.

6.
Show Your Youngsters How to Have "Pure" Fun.

The world tries to persuade our children that drinking, doing drugs, wild parties, and having sex outside of marriage are fun. Moreover, there's the message that if teens don't take part, they are weird, dumb, or socially inept. It's up to us parents and the church to show children that there is such a thing as "pure" fun, where laughter and good times aren't predicated on illicit behavior.

We find out what our children like to do, and then we do these things as a family or invite their friends to join us or even other families.

"We want your minds and bodies to be healthy and your souls right with God," we explain to our daughters.

Of course there are skirmishes, and sometimes our rulings disappoint the girls. Our daughters sure know how to try us emotionally, but even then we feel it is worth the struggle. Although they don't come right out and say so, our attitude and these times of pure fun are a relief to them.

We can only pray that in the long run they will be glad we hold the Word as the standard; we hope it will be their strength long after we are gone.

7.
Is Dating Necessary?

While our church does not sanction dating per se, the converted teen group does do fun things in groups. This provides safety from situations that lead to sin. In other conservative Christian circles, "courtship" is gaining popularity as parents see the fallacy of dating and the value in God's guidance in the selection of mates.

8.
Emotional Involvement Can Be Bad.

I tell my daughters not to get emotionally involved with a boy (you don't have to date to get emotionally involved). First, you waste time that could be spent enjoying a brotherly friendship or gaining a closer relationship with God (doing service projects, for example). If you are too young for marriage, such an intimate relationship is not ready to be formed, and you expose yourself to temptation.

This whole attitude takes discipline, sacrifice, and a mature Christian heart.

9.
NO DATING UNTIL EIGHTEEN.

We have a different view of dating at our house. My husband and I believe that dating puts an extreme amount of pressure on teenagers, pressure that most of them are not ready to handle. Our solution has been to delay dating one on one until age eighteen. Before then they can go out in groups, have friends over, or go to their friends' houses, but no one-on-one-out-in-the-car-alone until age eighteen.

The real purpose of dating is to look for a mate, but teenagers are not ready to think about that until their teen years are almost over. There are so many other things they need to concentrate on at this age, and getting too serious about one person too young is distracting. Dating detracts from seeing members of the opposite sex as friends and from schoolwork, and that's just for starters. The older the teens are, the wiser they will be about making choices, including dating.

10.
NO DATING ALONE UNTIL SIXTEEN.

My daughter wanted to go steady with a boy from school when she was just fourteen. She wanted to go places with him and be alone with him. Instead of forbidding her to do this, I sat down and explained the dangers of being alone with a boy at her age. She didn't totally believe what I was saying—her Robbie is a knight in shining armor to her— but I did tell her she could be with him as long as they were in a group. "And when you're sixteen, you can officially date."

11.
BE INVOLVED IN YOUR CHILD'S DATING.

"*M-o-o-m*, you're not going with us, are you?" groaned fifteen-year-old Ashli when I told her we were accompanying her boyfriend and her to the bowling lanes.

"No, you and Jeff are going bowling with your dad and me," I explained.

"He'll think I'm a baby if my parents go on our date," she whined.

"That's just the point, Honey," I admitted. "Your father and I don't want you dating alone until you're at least seventeen. But we don't mind you liking one boy over the others and, as long as you're with us, his family, or some group of people that includes adults, you can be together. How's that?"

Three guesses what her response was. I just smiled and reminded myself who the parent was.

12.
JUST BECAUSE THEY'RE CHRISTIANS DOSEN'T MEAN YOU CAN TOTALLY TRUST THEM.

Just because a boy is a professing Christian and comes from a strong Christian family is no guarantee that all is well when he begins dating your daughter. Our daughter came to us in tears one night when Gary tried to get her to undress for him. When she protested, he said, "It's okay. We're both Christians. God made sex and wants us to enjoy it."

Because we had spoken frankly with her about keeping herself pure until marriage and the teen group at our church stresses the same thing, she knew Gary's argument was a bad one. Even so, it scared her that she had to wrestle with him a little.

"I see now why you've warned me not to be alone with a boy in a place where I can't get away or get help," she told us. This happened in his home when his parents were away, so she was vulnerable.

She learned a sad lesson, but fortunately, she learned it without further tragedy.

13.
LET YOUR CHILDREN SEE DISAGREEMENTS
WITH YOUR SPOUSE.

I grew up in a healthy, middle-class home, and my parents never argued in front of my brothers and me. Consequently, when I got married I was baffled by the disagreements that arose between my wife and me. Over time I became disillusioned with the premise that love will conquer all. I felt betrayed by my parents for hiding the real evolution of relationships.

My struggle to get along with my wife was punctuated by heated disagreements, often carried out in front of the children. That led to more guilt on my part: I must be a bad husband if I want to argue with my wife; I must be a bad parent because I can't be the example my parents were and not fight with my wife in their presence.

Only through our church, and a series of marriage enrichment classes that helped me see that disagreements between husband and wife are normal and gave me tools for resolving those differences, was I able to understand the true meaning of relationship.

I want my kids to know it doesn't mean Mom and Dad are getting a divorce just because they raise their voices with each other once in awhile. Now that our two teenagers are getting ready to start dating, we don't want them to become disillusioned with love.

14.
MAKE THE RULES BEFORE THERE'S AN ISSUE.

Years before our daughter Melanie wanted to date, we talked about boy-girl relationships. We told her how we felt about her being alone with a boy, how we thought it best to wait until she was closer to eighteen or nineteen to do that, and, in the meantime, we had no objections to her being with groups of teenagers, boys and girls together. Melanie knew this was the road we would take before we even got there.

When she started to like one boy more than the others, she didn't fight us over the issue of being alone with him. She knew we had established the rule and that our rule was not based on our feelings for the boy.

15.
CONSIDER THE AGE OF YOUR DAUGHTER'S BOYFRIEND.

When Christy first wanted to date, we talked with her about age. "Until you go to college, we don't want the age difference between you and the boy to be more than two years," we told her. Of course, she reacted. "But Mom is eleven years younger than you," she declared.

"That's true, but an age difference between people who are in their thirties and forties is not as significant as it is when you're a teenager. You'll have to trust us on this."

It hasn't been easy to enforce this rule. Christy knows we don't want her getting too serious in her dating, which can happen if the boy is so much older than she.

16.
THERE'S NO MAGIC AGE WHEN DATING IS OKAY.

We told our three children that they would be allowed to date a boy/girl alone when we felt they were mature enough to handle it. We let them know it might not be the same age for all of them—no automatic allowing to date when they reached sixteen and so on. Setting this parameter before they reached the age of dating made it easier to guide them in this important aspect of their lives.

17.
HE'S NOT JUST DATING OUR DAUGHTER; HE'S DATING OUR FAMILY.

We had our sixteen-year-old daughter's twenty-year-old boyfriend visit our house many, many times before we allowed her to go anywhere with him alone. This was partly because she was a minor and partly because we had just endured many unhappy events in a year-long relationship she'd had with a non-Christian boy whose answer to a problem usually involved violence.

My husband, Sam, and I didn't want a repeat of that year, or worse, so we have gotten to know her new boyfriend well. We are surprised and relieved at how much Ben is like Sam. The more we get to know Ben, the more impressed we are. We treat him like a potential family member, which he is, and expect him to go by our household rules, which he does.

He knows, without being told, that his relationship with our daughter affects our entire family. We thank God that Ben is a Christian, very intelligent, and comes from a good family background.

18.
BE IN THE KNOW.

We always ask seventeen-year-old Theresa and her date where they are going, when they will be back, and who they'll be with. If we feel some part of the plan is unsafe, we tell them, and they come up with an alternative idea. My wife and I give them permission to go, with the parameters we have agreed on ahead of time. We expect the date to go as we have been told it will.

In the last six months, using these guidelines, we have had no major problems with Theresa's dating.

19.
WHY HER PARENTS SAID NO.

When our son Nick wanted to date a certain nice girl, her parents wouldn't let him. She is fourteen; he is seventeen. They have been friends for about two years, and the parents felt she was getting too emotionally involved and was too young to be getting love letters and sharing her thoughts on the phone.

The parents said, "We have the highest regard for Nick. If everything stays the same, he can court her in three years."

In the meantime they still see each other on a casual and friendly basis.

Although Nick is disappointed, he is using his time wisely to work and gain employment skills.

20.
"MY PARENTS WON'T LET ME," SHE SAYS.

Our fourteen-year-old daughter, Mandy, is still in eighth grade and not yet allowed to date. A few months ago she began receiving frequent phone calls from a boy she was not particularly interested in. He seemed immune to her not-so-subtle hints that she only wanted a casual friendship with him. When he asked her to go out with him, she told him, "My parents don't let me date yet. They're pretty protective, but I love them very much."

Sometimes parent-imposed boundaries can be helpful to a child trying to find her way through the dating scene.

DISCIPLINE

*He who spares his rod hates his son, but he
who loves him disciplines him promptly.*
PROVERBS 13:24

It had been a terrific day for the family, riding motorcycles together in Los Padres National Forest in south-
ern California. Amazingly, all six of our bikes had kept
running. Now as evening rolled in over the 1,724,000-
acre forest, Ken and I, Jim, David, and Lisa were loading
the bikes into the van and trailer. Only Terry, our oldest
son, was not there. He was still out riding with two of
his friends, but we knew they'd be in soon.

The sun set rapidly as shadows gulped hilltops, creating a bizarre patchwork of sun and shade across the valley floor. Our work completed, we sat still, enjoying the calm of the evening after a day of screaming bikes, dirt plastering our faces, and spills that tore our skin and clothes.

We waited. And waited. Soon the sun disappeared and dusk slipped into darkness.

"Where in the world are those kids?" Ken grumbled. "Terry knows they're to be back at camp before dark. It's a long way home."

The other father said, "Danny's always doing this to me, staying out later than he should."

We weren't too worried. After all, the guys, though fifteen, sixteen, and seventeen, were great riders who knew the territory well. And we knew where they had gone. Lockwood Trail was a treacherous, twenty-mile journey through the forest and over narrow, steep roads to a campground on the other side of the mountain.

Darkness now engulfed our camp. Stars blinked uncaringly a million miles away. There was no moon. It was so dark, we couldn't see our dog, Dusty, lying only twenty feet away. "Those guys," I mumbled. "Where are they?" Our ears strained against the silence to hear the welcome sound of an engine, but no sound came. It was past eight o'clock.

Nine o'clock blended into ten. Anxiety led to unspoken fear that something terrible had happened to the three boys out there in the primitive wilderness.

I prayed aloud, all of us bowing our heads: "Dear Heavenly Father, we come to You because we are helpless. There's nothing we can do for those boys who are in the darkness alone. Whatever has happened, please help them. Let them know You are near and protecting them. Guide them to us. In Jesus' name we pray, Amen."

By eleven o'clock it was cold. We put on jackets and huddled under blankets. Still no sound of the motorcycles broke the haunting silence.

Ken stood up. "It's time to notify the rangers that the boys are lost. They'll begin a search at daybreak." Did he mean we were leaving? None of us wanted to, but the valley would be freezing by morning, and what hope was there that the boys would be able to find their way back to the camp in the utter darkness?

Suddenly a sound burst through the air—the roar of an engine. We all leaped to our feet. "That's Terry's MX," Jim yelled. We listened, then another and finally the third bike was heard. They were coming!

It was a miracle that all three boys had made it over the narrow, winding roads that rose and fell through the mountain, where sometimes the path was only a few feet wide with a yawning cavern falling below.

"We were seventeen miles from camp when we realized we'd gone too far and needed to get back," Terry explained after many hugs and kisses and cries of relief. "Danny thought he knew a shortcut, but it turned out to be a dead end. By now we were on reserve fuel but we were able to coast downhill for miles. Glen ran out of gas first, then Danny, then me. We walked the bikes until we came to a campground where a nice old man gave us enough gas to get back here, except that we had to help him gather firewood for his family. We were now about six miles from camp, but it was pitch dark. We kept running into each other."

"I was so scared I wasn't breathing," Danny confessed.

"One time my bike hit a rock and I went down," Glen told us. "Terry rode over me and went down, too."

"I know this sounds crazy," Terry said, "but partway back it seemed as if a pair of hands were on top of mine, guiding my bike. I wasn't as afraid then, and I just relaxed and let the hands take me where they wanted. And here we are."

We all knew those "hands" were a direct answer to prayer.

The following week Terry came to us, excited, asking if he could go riding with some of his friends. Their families were going to a new motorcycle park near Palm Springs.

Ken said, "I'm sorry, Terry, but last week you broke one of the major rules of riding: Be back in camp before dark. No excuses. You three boys could have been killed. Easily."

"I know, Dad, but—"

"You're grounded from using your motorcycle for a month, Terry. Next time you decide to break a rule, such as not riding with a buddy, or wearing protective long-sleeved clothes and a helmet, you might not be so lucky. I want you to remember forever why safety rules are important."

"But Dad. . ."

Ken would not bend, and I was glad he didn't. Terry is still riding his motorcycle and has taught his own son, Jason, those same rules. Both have shared many hours of companionship on the trails—and they always get back to camp before dark.

1.
DISCIPLINE STARTS WAY BEFORE THE TEEN YEARS.

It is easier to discipline our daughter now because we set the groundwork early in her life. We trained her to know right from wrong as a child, coached her through her growing years, and now, as a teen, we are trying to manage her. We give her choices, and we give her reasonable consequences if she makes the wrong choice. However, the discipline has to fit the person. What works for one teen may not work for another. For instance, Debra loves talking on the phone, so we revoke all phone privileges for a week as one disciplinary consequence. We try to be consistent and firm with these consequences and trust they will build a wall of security around our teen and teach her that she needs to behave and choose responsibly.

2.
DISCIPLINE RIGHT NOW.

One evening my daughter Chelsey charged into her room and slammed the door shut, to emphasize to her father and me that she was not a happy camper. My husband stood up, got a screwdriver and hammer, and proceeded to take her door off the hinges. He then stored it in the garage.

There was no loud discussion—just the bottom line

from him: "You'll get the door back in a week." The message was clear.

3.

CORRECT WITH EXPLANATION.

When you correct your child, do so always with a loving explanation that is geared toward his understanding. "No, you can't take the car to Chicago," I told my son once, to his great disappointment. "You're not ready yet, just as a first-year medical student is not ready to perform brain surgery. The 'training' isn't completed. How about going, instead, to Bloomington for the afternoon? . . ."

4.

"THAT BEHAVIOR MERITS THREE BASKETS OF LAUNDRY. . . ."

Crude or dark humor, uncontrolled rage, or self-centered behavior that hurts someone else (plus other actions that require disciplining) is greeted with this statement: "That behavior means you have one (two, three. . .) basket of laundry to fold and put away."

This works well at all times and places—even in public—without too much embarrassment. All we have to do is look at Chad or Steve or Gary sternly and say, "Two baskets," and they know just what we mean.

5.
Explain Why Discipline Is Necessary.

"I hate it when you tell me to do something and never explain why," fourteen-year-old Lindsey hollered at me. "I want to know *why* I can't go to the dance. *Why* I can't start dating when all my friends already are. *Why* I have a dumb curfew on a Saturday night."

When I started to open my mouth, she continued, cutting me off. "It's ten times easier to go along or obey when I know why, Mom."

6.
Post a Chart of Rules.

There are certain teenage behaviors my husband (Mr. Marshmallow) and I (Wicked Witch of the North) cannot abide. Talking back, sneaky behavior, and name calling are just three. When our oldest child turned thirteen, she challenged every form of discipline we tried: grounding, time-outs, extra dishes, no phone, no make-up, no hair spray. Nothing worked with her. By then we had another teenager who was also determined to do things his way.

We called a family council and discussed what should be our family rules. They ranged from not eating in the living room to staying out past curfew. Then we let our teenagers assign consequences if these rules were broken. They chose tougher penalties than my husband and I would have, which surprised us.

The "Chart of Rules" is posted on a prominent wall in the pantry, near the crunchy peanut butter, for all to see. The excuse "I didn't know" is a thing of the past. Of course, the rules are broken, though not nearly as often, but there's no horrendous hassle about what to do about it. The kids just "get it over with," as they say.

7.
TRY IT ONCE — A FIRM RULE.

My daughters have been finicky eaters from the time they were toddlers. Thus, my wife and I were forced to come up with this rule: "Try it once. If you don't like it, you don't have to eat it again, not ever again if you don't want to." This rule is still in effect now that they've reached their teen years, and they pride themselves on being able to make their own "mature" decisions, as they call them. Sometimes they end up liking "gross stuff" because they give it a second chance on their own, without pressure from us. After all, I can't think of the last time I ate brussels sprouts!

8.
ONLY ONE "BORING"
FAMILY EVENT A MONTH IS REQUIRED.

On going to Grandma's, family reunions, weddings, and other "boring family things," the rule for Tim is this: Attend at least one function a month. Since we have a large family, these affairs are usually planned far enough in advance so that he can "schedule"—according to his boredom level—work, ball games, or absolutely-essential-that-I-attend school activities. We've taught him, though, to be polite enough to ask those who attended how things went: "Who was there?. . .What did you eat?. . .Did Uncle George get on his World War II soapbox?"

9.
INAPPROPRIATE TV IS. . .INAPPROPRIATE.

Many television shows are inappropriate for my kids to watch—but I need to explain why. Those programs that are questionable, I watch with them and make sure to put in my two cents at every opportunity. Jessica and Brandy end up quoting me to their friends—a lot. And their friends will call them and ask what I think of such-and-such a show.

An adult explanation works.

10.
THE STOPWATCH QUELLS GROANINGS.

All I have to do to get groans from my children is to say something like, "Don't leave your shoes on the stairs. Take them to your room."

Their response? "Aw, Mom, we don't have time."

When they say that, I get the stopwatch and time the seconds it takes for them to do the job right, even when they're poking along. It never fails to amaze them how little time it actually takes to do things the right way. It's become almost a game around our house now. "Oh, no," they'll shriek, "here comes Mom with her stopwatch."

11.
I'M FOLLOWING IN MY MOM'S FOOTSTEPS.

My mother was a single mom with eight kids. I was her natural daughter; the other seven were foster children. Here are "Momma's Rules":

(1) You *will* get a 3.0 GPA unless you have proven you can do better;

(2) You *will* play a team sport or be in at least one group activity such as choir, a musical or play, debate team, and so on;

(3) You *will* get a part-time job and pay for all your own needs unless it is discussed with me first;

(4) You *will* go to church once a week;

(5) You *will* help with the chores as a member of the team, or you will not eat or have laundry done—period.

How did we turn out? All eight made it through school. Only one got pregnant, had the child, kept it, and still graduated from school a semester early. All eight kids are college or Bible college graduates. All are Christians and vital parts of their communities. There are twenty-seven grandkids.

Momma is now seventy-three. Retired, yes? *No!* Momma now takes in three teenage foster boys at a time, the ones who have already been through the system. These are usually hard kids ready to pick the cell of their choice in prison. She has amazing success. "Here are The Rules," she tells them. And they listen.

12.
KNOW WHAT YOUR CHILD IS READING.

My mom always read any book before allowing me to read it. She would then put a rating inside the cover so she could remember if I could read it or not. When I was thirteen I wanted to read *Gone with the Wind* so badly that she decided I was ready. I read that book in four days because I was so afraid she would change her mind.

Now, with my teenage daughter, I do the same thing. As much as possible, I only want her reading books that will be good for her morally and spiritually.

13.
ESTABLISH FAMILY PRINCIPLES.

If your family operates on stated principles, there's less need for unpleasant discipline. Children know what's expected of them. Here's what we have posted in our kitchen:

(1) We serve the Lord.
(2) We respect other people.
(3) We fulfill our obligations whether we want to or not.
(4) There will be responsibilities, privileges, and consequences.
(5) Sometimes life isn't fair.

14.
DON'T UNDERMINE EACH OTHER'S AUTHORITY.

There are times when I think my wife is too hard on our daughter, but I won't question her in front of Cari. Instead, I'll go to Gina later and say, "Don't you think you were too hard on Cari?" If she agrees, then we'll go to Cari together and explain why Gina did what she did. But I'm careful not to undermine her authority with our child.

15.
There Is a Cost to Having Privileges.

Sometimes we parents fail to teach our children that privileges come when responsibilities are carried through. We give kids too much without asking them to contribute in some way. This leads to spoiled children who have an unrealistic view that society owes them a living, as well as a fat bank account, fancy house, new car, and two vacations a year.

That old cliche says it best: There is no free lunch.

16.
There Are Always Consequences

My son has a friend whose mother is forever excusing his deliberately bad behavior. She says to him, "I know you didn't mean to do it. . . . It's okay. . . . You couldn't help it." But to the observer, it is obvious he did mean to do it, . . . His behavior was not okay. . . . And he could have helped stop the situation from happening.

I shudder to think of him as an adult because he has grown up without accepting the consequences for his behavior.

17.
IS IT GOOD TO HAVE A WORLD WITH NO GRADES, NO COMPETITION, NO SCORES?

At a recent PTA meeting at my daughter's school, it was suggested that a new system of teaching be implemented that would involve giving no grades and giving no scores for school sports. "We don't want our children to experience failure," one well-meaning teacher explained.

When the meeting was opened to discussion, I shocked the group when I stood and said, "I teach my daughter to fail." I heard the gasps but went on. "Failure is inevitable. It is part of life. I would rather teach my daughter how to fail than have her become a failure. There is a difference."

Competition spurs us to reach new goals. Grades affirm we are learning. Scores reward effort. My daughter will not always reach the goals she sets for herself, or make the grade she studies for, or score the points she strives for. However, I will teach her, in that failure, that she is really a winner because she tried, and it is in the trying, the struggling, the reaching, that we attain our highest human potential.

18.
WORK AS A TEAM WITH YOUR SPOUSE.

My wife and I talk about family problems and search for their solutions together. We agree on family rules and how to enforce them, and we let our teens know of changes in policy together. We keep each other informed about what our teens tell us and check with each other when they ask to do something so that they can't get permission from one of us when they know the other will say no.

Being parents works a whole lot better when you do it as a team.

19.
HOW TO KEEP YOUR CHILDREN FROM BEING "MOTHER DEAF."

When my boys reached their early teens, they became "mother deaf": When I would ask them to do something or reprimand them, they would pretend they had not heard me. I became frustrated and often yelled at them. I did not like being this way, and no one else liked it, either.

My pastor suggested my husband get more involved. "Let him give the orders and decide consequences for disobedience," he suggested. (He said that ten is actually a good age for having the father take over a son's discipline.)

Ted agreed, and the boys had no problem responding to their dad. He was a guy like them, and because they were teenagers, they were starting to pull away from me and wanted to relate more to him. Now, I only help carry out the plan and have more opportunity to just enjoy my boys' company.

20.
RULES ARE FOR EVERYWHERE.

"Dad, Ginny's mom has rented a movie for us to watch," our daughter Christie said to me over the telephone. She was spending the night at Ginny's house. "Is it okay for me to stay and see it?" she continued.

I said, "What is it rated?"

She answered, "PG-13."

"Christie, you know we don't watch PG-13 movies."

"I know, but Ginny's mom is going to be in the room watching with us."

Ginny was listening in on another phone and said, "We promise to turn it off if there's anything bad in it."

"As soon as it goes by, you're going to turn it off? That will be too late, I'm afraid."

In the end, however, I gave in, leaving a final message: "Christie, you know what your mother and I expect of you."

"Yes, Dad."

Christie called back in less than ten minutes. "We've turned it off," she reported. "You were right; it's awful. Even Christie's mom thinks it's bad."

FRIENDS

If. . .your friend who is as your own soul, secretly entices you, saying, "Let us go and serve other gods,". . .you shall not consent to him or listen to him.

DEUTERONOMY 13:6,8

"Jim, you need to talk to your friend, Ron," Ken told our son. "He's got a bad temper, and I've caught him twice trying to take tools from my garage."

I agreed with Ken's assessment. I'd seen the boy's temper in action and was pretty sure he was the one who'd taken a five-dollar bill I'd left on the kitchen counter that afternoon, though I had no proof.

"You must be mistaken, Dad. Ron's a little hotheaded, but he's a good guy. And he wouldn't steal from you."

"If you don't talk to him about it, Jim, I will, and if he doesn't straighten up, then he won't be allowed to come over here."

A few days later Ron found Ken and me in the kitchen. "Jim tells me you don't like me," he began boldly. He stood with his hands on his hips, a smile on his lips.

"It isn't that I don't like you," Ken told him. "I don't like the way you act. When you come into this house, I want you to treat it like your own and not steal anything."

Ron stopped coming to our house. A few weeks later he and Jim got into trouble with the law. He was not a good friend.

1.
To Have Good Friends, You Have to Be a Friend.

We told Alisa that having good friends doesn't happen by accident but by mutual consideration and effort. Making friendship a priority means affirming those relationships with acts of unselfishness, while allowing your friends their personal space. You must go outside of yourself to be someone who will attract the right kind of friends.

2.
HAVE TEENS MEMORIZE IMPORTANT TRUTHS.

At the supper table, we memorize Scripture verses and phrases I make up that I hope my daughters will remember. "Evil company corrupts good habits," is a translation of 1 Corinthians 15:33. Two of my own "gems," as I call them, are the following: "Friends are made by many acts; they can be lost by just one" and "True friends are like diamonds, precious and rare. False friends are like pebbles; they can be found anywhere."

3.
NEVER TRY TO PICK YOUR CHILDREN'S FRIENDS.

You can botch a good relationship with your teen by interfering with his choice of friends. Don't even express opinions—he can read you like a book. (However, there is an exception to this rule: If his friends lead him into an immoral or illegal situation, you as parents have to step in.) Teens are desperately in need of peer acceptance and friendship.

4.
A Lesson Learned Is a Lesson Remembered.

While your heart aches when your child is betrayed by a fair-weather friend, pray that the experience will teach him to choose a better companion next time.

5.
Never Berate Your Child in Front of His Friends.

One day I got bold and asked my seventeen year old, "What's the worst thing I do as a parent?" I fully expected to have to pack my bag and move out, but he surprised me by having few complaints. "The *worst* thing you do, Dad," he said at last, "is you put me down in front of my friends. You're always saying something about my clothes or my attitude or that my hair is too long. You do it over and over, and it makes me feel like a baby."

6.
Don't Tease Your Teen In Front of Her Friends.

My daughter begged me with tears in her eyes not to tease her in front of her friends. "Especially about boys," she emphasized. "It is so uncomfortable. I hate it."

I quickly agreed to the simple request.

7.
We Don't Choose Their Friends.

Right now our children are open to our suggestions regarding friends, and they have made wise choices. But we don't choose their friends for them. Because of their personal relationship with the Lord and the respect they have for us as parents, Matt and Janice have chosen friends whose values are very close to our own. I have been amazed as I have seen the Holy Spirit work in their lives and lead them to make or withdraw from friendships.

I pray a lot!

8.
MAKE CHRISTIAN FRIENDS AVAILABLE.

When our family moved for the first time, we left an urban neighborhood (where my family lived next door) for a rural one. However, it didn't take long for our daughters, Janey and Diana, to make friends. Unfortunately, most of the neighborhood children were unsupervised because their parents were at work or asleep. Since I wasn't working, I encouraged my daughters to invite their friends to our house so I could get to know them and supervise the activities. In retrospect, that was a good plan I should have made into a rule.

Eventually, the other kids began to ask if my daughters could go to their houses. That request seemed only fair. I let them go for an hour or so. Then, as I became comfortable with the practice and busied myself with things I wanted to do in my new house, the times grew longer and longer. Before I realized it, I lost touch with what Diana and Janey were doing.

Just four months after our move, Janey spent the night with her new friend, Kirsten. Later, I found out they'd walked to Kirsten's boyfriend's house after midnight and climbed in his bedroom window. Although they had only sat on the bed and talked (so they said), I was horrified that Janey had participated in such covert and potentially dangerous behavior. We never let her spend the night with Kirsten again.

9.

GIVE YOUR CHILD FREEDOM
OF CHOICE OVER FRIENDS.

I have learned that one of the wildest, weirdest-looking kids I know is, at heart, not a bad kid at all. My hasty judgment made my son feel bad because I didn't trust him to choose good friends. I should have remembered the Lord's pronouncement to the prophet Samuel (1 Samuel 16:7): "For the LORD does not see as man sees; for man looks at the outward appearance, but the LORD looks at the heart."

10.

ASK QUESTIONS ABOUT
YOUR TEEN'S BEHAVIOR.

Our eighteen-year-old daughter has two best friends, both males and both gay. The three of them spend a lot of time together. When we learned these young men were gay, we talked with Laura about them, explaining our position on homosexuality, that we thought it was wrong and contrary to God's desires. Though we had never advocated being antagonistic toward those who practice this lifestyle, we wanted her to be careful not to be influenced by them.

Because our relationship with Laura has been strong enough through the years to talk about anything, this was no exception. Both my wife and I discussed these young men with her and how we were concerned that she would be enticed into this behavior.

"Don't worry, Mom and Dad," she said. "I'm not gay. I like guys. Mike and Dan are just good friends of mine."

While we did urge her to be aware of how deviant behavior can often be tempting, we knew we could not, at her age, demand she give up these friendships. This has become a major issue of prayer with my wife and me now. When we're not with Laura, we know that God is, and our prayer is that He will enable her to see the danger in being friends with people who deliberately sin.

11.
It's Okay to Say No.

I'm careful not to let my teenage daughter, Tracey, spend the night with a friend who is, in my mind, questionable. If I haven't been in that home and I don't know the rules of that home, I don't let her go.

12.
WE'RE NOT ALWAYS AS SMART AS WE THINK WHEN JUDGING OUR KIDS' FRIENDS.

There were two teenage friends of my daughters that I enjoyed seeing. They were polite. They asked about my life. They came from respectable families. Then one day, when I was commenting favorably on their manners and conduct, my oldest girl, Cynthia, told me the truth: "Mom, even though they're my friends, they're not as good as you think they are. Julie's been caught shoplifting more than once, and Diana is a liar."

I stared at her, embarrassed at my ability to be snowed by such "charming" teenagers. Then my parental reasoning kicked into gear, and I said to Cynthia, "If these girls are so bad, why are you friends with them?"

She saw the point, and within a month, neither girl came around anymore.

13.
CHRISTIAN FRIENDS CAN BE THE WORST INFLUENCES

As parents, we have to be careful of our children's Christian friends. I hate to say that, but there are many kids raised in Christian homes who easily fall to temptation. When they do and still claim to love the Lord, they are a terrible example to other Christian kids.

Parents, know *all* of your children's friends, Christian or otherwise.

14.
MAKING NEW FRIENDS AFTER MOVING CAN BE DANGEROUS.

Our daughter Cheryl was unhappy when we moved from the West Coast to the Northeast. She missed her friends tremendously and didn't even try to make new ones in our new neighborhood. Eventually, though, Cheryl started spending time with several teenagers who lived down the street who were older than she. I was concerned they were not steady, and I warned her of my feelings. Cheryl just shrugged off my concerns.

One night she sneaked out of the house to meet these kids. They went to the nearest Kmart, just to bum around, not being smart enough to realize that when three teenagers show up at two o'clock in the morning wearing long coats with big pockets, every clerk is on the alert, and security cameras easily pick up their activities because there are so few people around.

The end of the story is that the three of them stole some CDs, watches, and cameras. They were caught and put in jail for the night. I received a parent's worst phone call: "Mrs. James, this is the police department.

We have your daughter in custody."

Cheryl was scared silly in jail. Later, when she had to appear in court, she was terrified she'd be sentenced to more time in jail. The judge, though, took into account this was her first offense and ordered her to take a shoplifting course. She had to pay for it herself—seventy-five dollars. "If you finish the course and pass it," the stern judge told her, "this episode won't go on your record."

Cheryl was grateful for that gesture because she wanted to enter the military after high school graduation and couldn't have with a felony on her record.

The course consisted of reading material and answering essay questions which were then sent to a company in New York to be graded. Cheryl had to take her results to court and give the judge a record, which she faithfully did.

She passed the course, and her record is clean, but it was a traumatic lesson to her in choosing friends and allowing them to influence her.

15.
GIVE YOUR KIDS
THE BENEFIT OF THE DOUBT.

I let my children know I trust them to choose appropriate friends, ones who will not try to persuade them to do inappropriate things. They appreciate this trust and, so far, have not disappointed me.

16.
SHOW APPROPRIATE BEHAVIOR
TO YOUR CHILD.

Our daughter Lynne had a friend who "sassed" her mother. The first time we heard her do this, we said nothing to Lynne. However, after the second time, we talked to our daughter. "Did you hear how she spoke to her mother? How do you feel about that?"

This opened up a discussion on what behavior is appropriate and what is not. Having seen how unattractive sassing can be, Lynne got the point more dramatically than if we had just told her, "Don't ever sass us."

17.
IT'S HARD TO CRITICIZE
CHURCH FRIENDS.

Our son has a close friend at church. Whenever he spends time at Perry's house, he comes home short-tempered, rude, and hyperactive. "You're acting like Perry," we tell him. Gradually, he's beginning to see the faults in his friend's behavior. However, since he still wants to be with Perry, we have the boys at our house more, so we can monitor and control the situation.

18.
SHE COULDN'T JUST TAKE OUR WORD FOR IT.

When our family made the first major move of our lives, my husband and I were slow in finding a new church home. Kelly, our oldest daughter, made friends who quickly got her into trouble. They taught her new and different things, and she was curious.

Six months later, her new friends' influence and the increasing distance between us as parents and child were terrifying us. I searched out a nearby church similar to the one we had left before we moved. With a trembling voice and tears in my eyes, I talked to the minister about my concern for Kelly. He invited us to the church's Wednesday night dinner that week and asked one of the girls in the youth group to introduce Kelly to everyone and show her around.

Kelly became part of the youth group that night. Being with a good and moral peer group with the same basic values that we have taught her has made her a stronger person. In fact, last Christmas Eve she became a Christian. It was the most wonderful Christmas present we'd ever received.

19.
BAD DAY AT SCHOOL? LOOK TO FRIENDS.

When my daughter, Lindsey, gets off the school bus in the afternoon, the expression on her face says it all. Smile and slight bounce in her step—status with friends is status quo. Sullen look or pout and dragging her feet—friend crisis!

Even though she may tell me, at first, that her "down" attitude is because she has too much homework or a paper due the next day, it is really her friends that "rule" and "rock" her emotions.

Knowing this about Lindsey helps me cut to the quick of the problem before she digs too deep a hole for herself. The sooner the crisis is pacified, the sooner she can resume her other roles in life—that of daughter, sister, and student.

20.
TRY TO STAY OUT OF YOUR TEEN'S RELATIONSHIPS.

Since I mostly work from home, my presence is always felt. My boys bring their friends home *a lot*—for after-school homework sessions, TV movies, and to stay for supper. One boy has spent three Christmas Eves and Christmas mornings with us because his mom is busy looking for a new husband.

Sure, my kids bring home any number of boys I

don't care for, but I figure my being here, and stating my opinions, is a better learning tool than stomping around like an old clodhopper and saying, "Stay away from that boy!"

By allowing Jeremy and Sam to "hang" with the so-called undesirables, they soon see for themselves why that name gets attached to certain kids. Sometimes the "un" is dropped because they go with us to church, learn some manners, and participate in our family's "What did you do today?" chats around the supper table. These experiences turn them around.

21.
THEY MAY NEED FORGIVENESS.

Because we are a family of modest means, my daughter, Amy, has worked at Wal-Mart for some time to buy and pay for a Ford Escort. A year ago, her best friend took Amy's car without permission and totaled it. Amy was devastated because she had no collision insurance and no money to get another car. She told kids at school what had happened. The best friend twisted the story to make Amy look like the guilty party. Their friendship, which had begun in the third grade, hit the rocks.

My husband and I counseled Amy, after she'd cooled down, to talk with her friend and make amends. Amy didn't think she could do it. We told her a friendship is worth saving and means more than a car. "You need to accept Julie back into your life unconditionally," we urged her.

It wasn't easy, but Amy did just that, and so did we. We had Julie to the house, and we talked with her and hugged her and let her know, even though she'd made a bad mistake, we still cared about her.

Over time this friendship was restored, and in the end, Julie helped Amy pay for another car.

22.
COMMUNICATE WITH PARENTS OF YOUR CHILDREN'S FRIENDS

It's really important to keep tabs on your kids—whom they're with, where they go, and what they do. One way is to have a strong support system between the parents of your children's friends and you. My son Joey has a good friend, and even though we trust them together, we keep up with their doings through Joey's parents, and they with us. We never leave the details of their being together hanging in the air or to chance. I will not let my son spend a lot of time with friends without having this communication with other parents.

MESSY ROOM

For conciliation pacifies great offenses.
ECCLESIASTES 10:4

It was Saturday. Time for the dreaded rounds to check the condition of my children's bedrooms. I took two aspirin, straightened my shoulders, and marched head-long into the fray.

Lisa's room was not bad; David's was a disaster, and Terry's was only a little better. Jim's room could be brought up to my standards in a half-hour or so.

I was surprised to find Jim at the scene of the crime. The other kids had skedaddled, full knowing, though, that they'd have to face the music sooner or later that day.

"Are you going to work on your room, Jim?" I asked him.

"Can't. I have to get to baseball practice."

"When you get home then?"

"I'll be late. Some of us guys are going to Craig's house to help his dad put in a patio."

I smiled. "That's commendable, Jim, but you know that Saturday is the day for cleaning your room. This is a rule in our house. It's important not to let clutter get out of control—"

He stopped my lecture by silently taking my hand and leading me out of the room, across the hallway, down the stairs, and to the garage door which he opened.

I stared at my husband's kingdom, where he diligently worked at keeping our home and property in tiptop condition, where he spent hours with the boys and Lisa tinkering with their motorcycles and bicycles, where every square milli-inch of space was covered with "something." The word clutter could not begin to describe the chaos.

I gave Jim a weak smile. "Your father is beyond help, I'm afraid, but I have high hopes for you, Jim. You could be neat if you tried."

"I'll see you tonight," he promised with a grin. "My room will be cleaned up."

The sun burst from behind a dark cloud and flooded the garage with brilliant light. I'm sure I heard an angel choir singing just beyond our driveway.

1.
EVERYTHING OFF THE FLOOR ONCE A WEEK.

My daughter was the queen of the messy room. End of contest. Her room looked like the inside of a clothes dryer with clothes everywhere. If you fell down in her room, you would probably get up with two or three outfits on.

The solution that finally worked (somewhat) was to specify that Jenny get everything off the floor once a week. I let her pick the day she wanted to do this horrendous deed.

"What do I need to do?" she asked.

"Floor cleared, linens changed on the bed, dresser dusted. Then, and only then, do you get your allowance."

The rest of the week I just request that she keep her door shut.

2.
SOME TEENS WILL NEVER BE ORGANIZED.

Lauren needed to be organized. That was the simple solution, as I saw it, to getting her to keep her room picked up. Because I was born organized, I have difficulty understanding why others defy nature. Lauren has taught me once and for all that folks are different.

To help organize Lauren, I bought a book that showed

how to be organized in just five days. Five days. Just what "we" needed. I read the book. Lauren read the book. Did she miraculously become organized? *No!* She stayed the same. I, on the other hand, am more organized than ever.

3.
GET TEENS TO MAKE
A TO-DO LIST.

Maybe it's seeing a list of things on a piece of paper that has helped Max clean his room better than if I just give him a bunch of verbal commands, but lists definitely work. I got used to making out the list myself, and he got used to following it, as only a fourteen year old can who'd rather be playing baseball. In short, there was no enthusiasm for the job.

Then I came up with a brilliant idea: Let Max make his own list. The first few times he did it, the list was cryptically short: "Clean room." With a little kind encouragement from me, his father, he began to be more specific: Put video games on shelf. Hang up clothes. Take leftover food to garbage.

I'd say it's a natural desire to plan his own activity that has changed his I-don't-care-if-I-ever-clean-my-room attitude to Okay-if-I-have-to-do-this-I'll-make-the-decisions-what-to-do attitude.

I do make him post his list in the kitchen pantry, so I can see it, and he knows I can see it.

4.
IT'S NICE TO COME HOME TO A CLEAN ROOM.

When my fifteen-year-old daughter and I were not on good terms and growing away from each other, I decided to become more of a friend and mother her less, though not be less of a mother. I thought of things I could do for her as a friend who understood she was going through a tough emotional time. I wanted to show her that I loved her and cared about her well-being. One way I did this was by cleaning her room.

At first she was suspicious of my intentions until I told her I just wanted to make her feel better. By the way, we get along great now that she is eighteen, and she cleans the room herself, most of the time.

5.
ON THE WEEKEND
THEY MUST CLEAN THEIR ROOMS.

I don't make a major issue over messy rooms during the week. I just close my eyes and hold my breath when I walk by my sons' rooms. However, when the weekend comes, it's time to clean up. Once a week the condition of their rooms has to please me—not to my level of clean, but an acceptable standard. My sons vacuum, dust, and change the sheets on their beds.

They remove food and drink. I try to make them realize the condition of the carpet and furniture tops is important. I'd like them to make their beds every day, but I don't insist on it.

6.
A SEMIORDERLY ROOM IS FINE WITH ME.

While some parents say they just close the door on a messy room, I can't do that. I don't want my children going through their entire lives being disorganized. Where better to learn than at home that it's necessary to keep your area picked up and clean!

7.
A CLEAN ROOM GRANTS THE PRIVILEGE OF GOING SOMEWHERE SPECIAL.

We expect our daughters to clean their rooms on the weekend, that time of the week when they often have somewhere special to go. Tracey knows that if her room is a disaster, she won't be allowed to go with the kids from church or with friends to some anticipated activity.

8.
I Only Allow So Much Mess; Then It Must Be Cleaned.

I don't go into my kids' rooms unless I need to. They deserve this privacy and respect since they don't come into my room without permission. Sometimes I walk by Aaron's room, and it looks like four tornadoes have gone through in the space of five minutes. That's when I say, "This room needs to be cleaned by Saturday. If it isn't, a privilege will be taken away, or there will be a consequence."

9.
Give Them a Reason to Keep Their Rooms Clean.

Our daughter's room was always a disaster until she got a kitten, which we allow her to keep in her room. She knows she doesn't dare leave her clothes in a pile on the floor: The kitten likes to snuggle among them and might get stepped on. She doesn't leave food and drink around either: The cat eats what isn't good for it or spills the drink.

I am amazed at the difference one small, furry creature has made in my daughter's attitude toward keeping her room picked up.

10.
INCENTIVES ENCOURAGE RESPONSIBILITY.

My son knows that if his room isn't cleaned to my standards by Saturday afternoon at four, he won't be able to use the car that night or for the next week. Another consequence when he neglects his responsibility is that he is unable to go to the mall.

11.
DON'T LET THE MESS GET OUT OF CONTROL.

I find it's better to keep our son's room moderately picked up than to let it get to be a jungle—and then try to get him to straighten it up. One incentive toward achieving this goal involves our computer. Jeff is allowed thirty minutes a day on his computer. If he keeps his room neat, to his mother's and my standards, which are as loose as we can make them in good conscience, then he can have his thirty minutes. If his room is especially neat or he does extra chores around the house and yard, he is allotted more time. Of course, if the room is a disaster, computer minutes are taken away.

12.
GIVE KIDS A SAY
IN THE DECORATING.

"It's your room," I told my son and daughter. "Paint it any color you want. Put whatever you like on the walls." My son's room is pea green and depressing (to me); my daughter's room is sky blue. We discovered her artistic talent when she painted a rainbow on one entire wall. Both kids have hung up posters as well as dozens of pictures with hooks and nails. No longer can we say, as a punishment, "Go to your room." They love their rooms and spend a lot of time there.

13.
KNOCK BEFORE ENTERING
YOUR CHILDREN'S ROOMS.

It is a rule at our house for our children to knock before entering our bedroom, even if the door is open. I give them the same respect and knock before entering their rooms.

14.
Avoid Meltdown.
Decide What Doesn't Really Matter.

I used to think the world would stop turning if the beds weren't made. When I discovered that wasn't true, my stress load lessened. I concentrate now on those things that must be done, such as getting supper for my family, taking my daughter to the dentist to get her cavity filled, and making time for my husband.

15.
Organize Your Child's Room.

Simply put, have a place for everything. My daughter, at fifteen, can spell "organize" but she can't do it. So, I organized her room for her by making sure there was a place for everything: hangers in the closet for clothes, drawers in the dresser that opened easily, hooks for belts and hats, shelves for teddy bears, jacks for telephone and television, school supplies for her desk. She does a fine job keeping her room picked up. She just can't organize.

16.
TEENS SHOULD HAVE A SAY ON HOW THEIR ROOMS SHOULD LOOK.

I want my sons to take pride in their rooms. "Would you like to move the furniture? Have new wallpaper? Paint the ceiling fan?" They have each given me a list of "wants" for their rooms. If they've done something that deserves a special reward, I will get an item from their list as a surprise.

17.
ONCE A YEAR, HAVE A THOROUGH CLEANING.

On the first day of summer holidays, my children—ages eight, eleven, and fifteen—turn everything out of their rooms and do a thorough cleaning. That is the only activity allowed for that day. On this particular day the kids are still in a "school" mode and are not hanging loose like they are for most of their vacation. While they dread the day, they are usually surprised at the stuff they find, including, invariably, some long-lost treasures.

On that day the carpet is vacuumed and cleaned, walls and doors are washed where needed, windows scoured inside and out, and shelves and knickknacks dusted.

The end of the day brings a visit to their favorite pizza place to celebrate the beginning of summer vacation.

18.
I Want That Room Cleaned.

Nancy, age fourteen, is the world's messiest person. No doubt about it, she takes the prize. A few months ago, her room finally became more than I could stand. One fateful Saturday morning when she was babysitting, I went into her room to look for something. Big mistake! Every inch of floor space was covered with something. Under her bed were clothes, books, papers, candy wrappers, packages things came in, and so on, piled from the floor clear to the box springs.

Her father and I removed the mattress and box springs from her bed, put a *big* garbage bag in their place, and waited for her to come home. When she did, we informed her she could not leave her room, and the mattress and box springs would not be replaced, until that space was liveable again.

Was she furious! But I would not back down—I *wanted that room cleaned!* And clean it she did, over the next three hours amid loud groaning and moaning.

Happily, she has never let it get quite to that point again. Her room still gets messy, but not *that* messy, and when we say, "Clean your room," she does.

19.
Allowances Keep Rooms Tidy.

I stopped giving my children allowances when they graduated from high school, and that's when their rooms got messy. I had gone by a "you get paid for what you do," mindset before. But when they reached eighteen, with no allowance as incentive, they had little reason to be neat. So, I shut the doors to their rooms.

When folks came over and wanted to see the house, I'd open their bedroom doors with a warning: "Careful where you step; you could break an ankle in here!" The guests' reaction? "Your mom keeps such a beautiful house; why does your room look like that?"

It became their responsibility, not mine, to answer for the mess. People could see by the condition of the rest of the house that it wasn't *my* style to be a slob. I told my daughters, "If you choose to live like a pig, don't be surprised when people expect you to oink!"

20.
Make a To-Do List.

I write a list of things for my teens to do and have it waiting when they get home from school or when they get up in the morning. Such a list needs to be specific, so there is little or no room for misinterpretation: (1) Pick up your clothes and bring them to the laundry room (2) Dust the top of your dresser (3) Vacuum the rug in your room. They may look for loopholes or not do the entire job if it's too general.

I try to remember to tell them, as they leave for school or the night before, that they will have a list of things to do so they are mentally prepared and don't plan something else.

There has been very little or no fussing about helping around the house and cleaning their rooms. I think it may be because they can see a light at the end of the tunnel, an end to the list. I never add to it after they have seen it, and I don't overload them with chores. There is always tomorrow.

Sometimes they negotiate to trade jobs with each other. I try to stay out of such conversations and let them work it out.

21.
No Food or Drinks
in the Room.

We had relaxed the rule of no food and drink in Don's room. After all, he was sixteen going on seventeen. Surely he wouldn't want moldy food laying around or half-full cans of soda on the dresser where he could knock them over onto his girlfriend's picture.

An imminent visit from my mother caused me to rush into Don's room to be sure it was presentable. One look at the hungry fieldmouse nibbling on the cheese from last month's hamburger—not to mention the nearby half-eaten chocolate cupcake nestled against the tipped-over can of root beer that had stained the new carpet—and the rule went back into force. Immediately.

MONEY

Poverty and shame will come to him who disdains correction, but he who regards a rebuke will be honored.

PROVERBS 13:18

"I've found the perfect used car for David," Ken told me. "It doesn't look like much, but it runs well and has been maintained through the years."

"He'll be so excited," I answered. "Ever since he got his driver's license he's wanted his own car."

"It's got some dents and scratches," Ken warned me.

"I understand," I said, and I did. While I wanted my child driving a car that had fewer than a hundred dings on it and a paint job that could be identified as a specific color, Ken was only interested in how it managed mechanically.

"You found me a car?" David exclaimed to us an hour later when he came home from school and found an unfamiliar one sitting in the driveway. He was ecstatic. "How many miles does it have on it?" He went on to ask all the same questions Ken must have asked the owner, while I wondered how soon we could get it painted so it wouldn't be an eyesore in the neighborhood.

"I know you can't afford the entire price right now," Ken said to David, "but your mother and I are willing to advance you the money, and you can pay us back in weekly payments."

"That's great," David agreed. "Thanks, Dad, Mom."

"The down payment, though, is your responsibility. We know you've been saving for over a year, and you can be proud that you have enough to help buy your own car."

David just looked at us and didn't say anything.

"You do still have that three hundred dollars, don't you, David?" I asked. Surely he did; he'd just mentioned it to me a week before. He was proud he'd saved so much working at the pizza place.

"Uh, I did have the money. . .until a few days ago."

"What did you do with it?" Ken asked.

"Gave it to a friend."

"What?" both Ken and I exclaimed at the same time.

"He needed it. It was an emergency."

"Is he going to pay you back?" I asked.

"Maybe. I don't know. If he does, it won't be for awhile."

Ken let out a sigh of exasperation and looked up at the

sky. I felt a mixture of frustration and disappointment. I'd always appreciated David's generous spirit. He loved helping friends. His giving of himself and his resources was one thing that made him so special. In this case, though, he'd done a foolish thing.

It was no minor event that his dad had agreed to pay several thousand dollars for a car that he expected David to pay for himself eventually. Ken was big on personal responsibility, and I agreed with him. With four children all wanting cars, we just didn't have the money to buy each one what they wanted and not expect them to do all they could to help.

"David, I don't understand you," Ken began. "You knew you were going to be getting a car soon. You knew part of the deal that your mother and I help you with the payments was that you have the down payment."

"I know, Dad." David looked down at his feet.

"Then why on earth did you give away your money?" Ken's voice was rising. I felt almost sick to my stomach.

"Greg needed it, Dad."

"Why?"

"To buy a car to get him to Colorado."

"Oh, nice. Your friend wanted to go to Colorado—what, to go skiing?—and didn't have a car, so he found you and talked you into giving him—"

"Dad, wait," David interrupted him. "It wasn't a fly-by-night thing. He had a job there."

"Who is this friend of yours, David?" I asked.

"The youth pastor at church, Mom. Greg Lambert. You know him. He's been asked by a church in Colorado to start their youth program. Last week, just before he was going to leave, the engine went out on his old car. He sold his prize record collection to try to get the money to repair the engine, but it wasn't enough."

He paused, and I began to feel huge pangs of guilt for not trusting David's judgment. Ken looked uncomfortable, too.

"I gave him my three hundred dollars so he could go now and get there when they needed him. He said he'll send me the money as soon as he gets on his feet—and I'm sure he will."

I know I saw a tear in Ken's eyes. He clasped his arm around David's shoulder and gave him a shake. "Come on, Son, let's see how this baby runs."

Father and son got into the car. Both had big grins on their faces, and I had never been prouder of a child.

Money. What's it good for if not to help a friend?

1.

A JOB WELL DONE DESERVES A MONETARY REWARD.

I wanted my children to learn the valuable lesson that if you do a job well, your boss will reward you with a paycheck. On the other hand, if you do poorly, you'll hear about it. So I paid for grades: five dollars for As, three dollars for Bs, fifty cents for Cs. And my kids stayed on the honor roll straight through high school, though probably not because of the money. I'd always told them: "Dad's job is 'out there,' my job is to keep the house, and your job is school." By that line of reasoning, a paycheck made sense.

2.
DON'T COUNT EVERY PENNY
YOU GIVE YOUR CHILDREN.

We've never been averse to giving our children money. When they need something, as long as it's within reason and we can afford it, we get it for them. While they were growing up, we never gave allowances. And we didn't pay for chores. After all, their mother and I don't get paid for what we do around the house for the family, so neither should they.

Now that our boys are teenagers, we still see that they have money, but it's not much since they work and earn most of their expenses. They've worked at various jobs since they were old enough to have paper routes, and we've taught them the value of a dollar.

3.
SHOW TEENS HOW TO DISTRIBUTE MONEY.

Our teenage daughters receive money from babysitting and on special occasions from us and their grandparents. We've set up a bank account for each of them and have taught them the simple laws of banking. Any money that comes to them is divided three ways: one-tenth goes to the Lord as their tithe, most of what's left goes into the bank, and some is kept out for spending on whatever they want.

4.
SOME CHILDREN ARE MOTIVATED TO EARN MONEY.

My daughter doesn't care how much money she has or doesn't have, but my nephew is highly motivated to earn. He started working from an early age at whatever job would pay him something. Now he eagerly takes on extra chores. My sister sometimes withholds money from him as a form of punishment, and this is very effective. I've tried this approach with Cynthia, but it doesn't work with her or effect the change I want. She just isn't that interested in having money.

5.
PROVIDE MONEY FOR IMPORTANT THINGS; LET THEM WORK FOR THE FRIVOLOUS.

Our teenage son always spent his allowance before he was paid again, and then he would start whining for more money. Since I don't believe in paying for chores done around the house and property, I now see to it that Peter gets money for worthwhile activities—as long as he's done the family work he's assigned. If he wants spending money for what I call "unessentials," he must find a way to earn the money himself.

6.
TEACH THEM TO TAKE CARE OF THEIR OWN MONEY.

I don't want my children to have to depend on someone else handling their money. The day my twin daughters turned thirteen, I set up separate checking accounts for them. I showed them how to deposit money (on a field trip to the bank), how to withdraw, how to write a check, and how to balance the account at the end of the month. I explained interest and credit card use. I took them to a friend of mine who is a financial consultant and had her explain how to avoid serious debt.

I'm proud to say they both know how to handle money and enjoy doing so responsibly. On their eighteenth birthday I'm giving each of them a considerable sum, as are their grandparents, but I am confident they won't squander the money.

7.
ENCOURAGE SAVING FOR A SPECIAL WANT.

I never laugh at my son or treat it lightly when he comes to me, excited, and wants to buy something. Currently it's a CD player he's saving for. I respect his wanting one and his knowing he can't get the money from us.

While we don't pay for typical chores done for the family, we do pay for extra projects, as do a few of our neighbors. One woman has a lovely rose garden but has trouble bending over to weed. James earns a few dollars a week helping in her garden. We praise his industriousness and encourage him to work hard to achieve his goal.

Learning how long it takes to save money for a CD player will give him an idea of how long it will take to accrue the money for his first car. Now that will be a challenge!

8.
CLOTHES COST MONEY, SO TAKE CARE OF THEM.

When we go shopping for clothes, I've taught my daughters to look at the price tag before deciding they want something. Often it is shocking what a simple shirt or pair of slacks costs. At different times of the year I may say, "I can spend one hundred dollars on each of you for clothes. Remember that as you browse." They are learning how much money it takes to live nowadays.

9.
TEACH THEM ABOUT BARGAINS, SALES, AND GARAGE SALES.

Anyone who pays full price for clothes hasn't taken the time to shop around. My son, Bill, thought we could buy him all the things he wanted as well as needed. When he got to be a teenager, I began teaching him how to shop for bargains, check the newspaper for sales, and find great stuff at garage sales. Every Saturday morning we go out for a couple of hours and hunt for bargains. It's a great activity, and Bill's learning valuable lessons.

10.
EARNING THEIR OWN MONEY BUYS THEIR DESIRES.

I don't mind spending money on the necessities my teenager has—food, clothing, shelter, education, some entertainment—but I can't spend money on designer clothes, fancy cars, and dating expenses. Consequently, Todd began working a few hours a week for spending money from the time he discovered that fun costs big time.

Together we worked out a budget, and he eagerly

participated in its designations: 10 percent for church tithe, 15 percent for personal enjoyment, and 75 percent in the bank for the car he hopes to buy on his seventeenth birthday. We don't push him to work any set number of hours, but we do require that he allow himself plenty of time for school study, relaxation, and church attendance.

He's learning a basic principle of our household: You must work for what you have.

11.
LET THEM BUY WITH THEIR OWN MONEY WHAT YOU DON'T WANT TO PROVIDE.

Since becoming a teenager, our daughter no longer finds the nourishing lunches I pack satisfactory. "I need something hot," she declares.

"I'm providing you with a good lunch," I tell her. "If you want hot food, you'll have to buy it yourself."

"That's not fair; I have to eat lunch. I just don't want what you have at home."

"That's your choice."

The end result: Alicia buys her meals at school with babysitting money at least three times a week.

12.
Don't Pay for Chores.

While I don't pay my children for doing chores, I do reward them for work well done with little treats, eating out, or a special privilege.

13.
What Will Forty-Five Dollars Buy?

When my daughter complained that she didn't have enough clothes, I took her to the mall and gave her forty-five dollars and asked her to buy what she could with it. She came back with one pair of designer jeans.

I then took her to a discount store and gave her another forty-five dollars. She came back with a pair of jeans, two shirts, a purse, and a pair of earrings.

"Wow, Mom," she exclaimed, "I thought this store only sold junk. Was I ever wrong!"

14.
SHARE ADVICE WITH YOUR TEEN
ON HOW TO HANDLE MONEY.

My husband's millionaire uncle gave us some advice on how to invest in the stock market. We had been buying CDs for years but the interest rates kept getting lower and lower, and although the CDs were safe, so was a can buried in the backyard. Sam's uncle told us how he had invested two thousand dollars in a mutual fund thirty years ago, and now it was worth one hundred thousand dollars. Our daughters' ears perked up when they heard that.

Now, as our CDs mature, we roll them over into mutual funds, and we're seeing a steady increase in our earnings.

The girls follow our financial progress, too, and are learning the risks as well as the rewards of investing in the stock market.

15.
INVEST IN YOUR CHILD'S FUTURE.

We spend the majority of our extra money on our two sons. I'm not saying they get everything they want, but we'd much rather let Jeff and James go to Christian school and Christian camps and activities than buy something for ourselves that we really don't need, or go out to eat all the time. It's important to us, as parents, to invest our money as well as our time in our children's future.

16.
SHOW TEENS THE RESULTS
OF SQUANDERING MONEY.

When he turned nineteen, our oldest son wanted to move out of the house and get an apartment with two friends. Because he did not save his money, he's still living at home. His younger brother, Chris, at fourteen, sees his brother's frustration over money—in not being able to move out and in not being able to buy the things he wants.

Thus, Chris started keeping his own financial record in a notebook, just columns that show whom he worked for, how many hours he worked, how much an hour he made, the total earned, and amounts to go into tithe and savings. His goal is to buy his own car on his sixteenth birthday. He's well on his way—and he has his priorities straight. He always allows first for tithe and savings before spending.

17.
LET TEENS CONTRIBUTE
TO MAJOR TRIPS.

Our fourteen- and thirteen-year-old daughters each paid us back for 35 percent of the cost of a school trip to Yellowstone National Park. They paid us half of their baby-sitting income until their balance was paid off. While few of their classmates had to pay for any portion of the trip with their own money, we felt that helping to pay gave our daughters a sense of accomplishment and an understanding of the value of hard work and money.

18.
YOU WANT SOME?
GO EARN IT!

Both my daughters had part-time jobs from the time they were twelve when they started babysitting and caring for neighbors' pets. The money they earned was theirs to do with as they wished. I suggested, in the beginning, that they "blow" half and save half, and to make that seem less restrictive, I insisted they spend the entire first check on fun stuff.

Cari and Carla started savings accounts when they were thirteen, and by the time they wanted that first car, both had healthy down payments saved.

They were required to have a 2.5 GPA plus enough money to pay their share of the car insurance before each was allowed to get her driver's license—good incentive to stay on the straight and narrow *and* to work for what they want in life.

19.
SHOW CHILDREN HOW TO HAVE THE THINGS THEY WANT.

Our son has started to pick out his own clothing, shoes, and hairstyle. Now he even wants contact lenses! He usually picks high-ticket items which, even if we could afford them, we would not purchase.

"We'll pay for a certain level of personal grooming," we told him, "but if you want a particular brand of shoes or jeans that go over our budget, you'll have to use your own money to make up the difference."

This approach has made him stop and think. I've watched him time and again walk away from an expensive piece of clothing because he doesn't want to fork over his own money for it. He still makes silly purchases, but he is learning to make wise choices, too, and is complaining less about "not having what everyone else has."

20.
BIG MISTAKE —
DOING EVERYTHING FOR YOUR CHILDREN.

I liked being the kind of dad my kids could come to whenever they needed something. It made me feel worthwhile to know I was earning enough money to pay for all the things they needed and much of what they wanted, too. I never made my kids work. I paid for their college education and wouldn't let them have part-time jobs because I wanted them to enjoy the whole experience of college life.

My daughter survived my stupidity just fine. She works hard as a paralegal and handles responsibility easily. Her bank account is growing; she's paid off her car, and she rarely buys on impulse.

My son can't balance a checkbook. Money comes, and money goes in his life with the rapidity of a speeding bullet. He drifts from one job to another, seldom working anywhere longer than six months. His car is a junk heap, and his debts are mounting.

I wish now that I had taught him more about personal responsibility when he was growing up.

NEW FAMILY

Honor your father and your mother, that your days may be long upon the land which the LORD your God is giving you.

EXODUS 20:12

I dashed into the kitchen lugging a most important bag. I had just purchased designer jeans for our oldest son who, I knew, would be thrilled because they were what he'd been bugging us to buy him for six months. We couldn't afford them before, but now I'd found them on sale and had bought him not one but *two* pairs of the ugly things. Naturally, I eagerly anticipated his undying gratitude that he'd show by giving me the

Stepmother of the Year Award, maybe even the Step-mother of All Time Award, accompanied by a loving I'm-in-awe-of-your-shopping-skill kiss on the cheek.

I found sixteen-year-old Terry in the kitchen watching television and eating a huge bowl of orange sherbet with a soup spoon.

"Terry! Guess what I just bought for you! *Two* pairs of Twaddle jeans! Hurry up and try them on! I want to see how handsome you look! You can wear them on your date tonight with Tina!"

When Terry didn't jump for joy, or turn off the television, or even put down the soup spoon, I became worried.

"Are you ill?" I asked him.

He shook his head no.

"Aren't you excited about what I just said?"

He shook his head no.

"Two pairs of Twaddle jeans, right here in this bag." I rattled the bag to emphasize what I'd just said in case he'd gone deaf since that morning. "*Two* pairs." I punched the bag. "*Two* pairs just for you, oh adored son. Two pairs of your favorite designer jeans that you've been dying to have for six months. *Two* pairs!"

He sighed. He put down the spoon. He turned off the TV. He gave me the same look he would give an insane person.

"Nobody wears Twaddle jeans anymore. I wouldn't be caught dead in them. My friends would think I'm gay."

My heart sank. "But. . .but. . .they were on sale."

"That's why they were on sale: Nobody wears them anymore. Especially me and my friends."

I let the bag fall to the floor. I wanted to cry.

Terry smiled, and my world got a little better. "You

deserve the Mother of the Year Award."

My lower lip quivered. He had said Mother, not Stepmother.

"Thanks for trying," he added.

I walked to the silverware drawer and took out another soup spoon. I took the orange sherbet away from him and began to eat. What difference would two more pounds make on a woman who couldn't even buy proper clothes for her child?

1.
"JUST CALL ME S'MOM."

Jill, at fourteen, didn't know what to call me when I first married her father. Her mother had given her strict instructions not to call me Mom or even Mother, and that was fine with me because I wasn't her real mother. But at the same time, Jill didn't feel comfortable calling me by my first name, Sue. So I suggested she call me S'mom, an abbreviation for Stepmom. Jill loved the name and used it for two years, when she dropped it and began calling me Sue. I never questioned why; it just felt right to her, I guess.

2.
DON'T LET THE INSECURITIES OF THE FIRST WIFE DETER YOU FROM BUILDING A GOOD RELATIONSHIP.

My husband's first wife, Amy, hated it when Jim married me. She felt threatened, thinking I was going to try to take her place with their son. She filled Ricky's head with negative comments about the kind of person she thought I was. I had to work hard to bring down the barriers she put between us, so our relationship could begin and grow.

Ricky, at nine years of age, was a bright boy, and it wasn't long before he realized there was a difference between what his mother said and what I actually was. He's thirteen now, and we have a great relationship. (His mother, though, still doesn't like me.)

3.
MEET THE NEW DAD.

When my wife married again, she told me on the phone what a great guy her new husband was. While I was happy for her, I was not about to let our daughter, who lives with me, visit them until I'd met the guy myself. We arranged a dinner together, just us men, at a town midway between where we both live. After a three-hour time of sharing with Jack, I knew he'd be a good influence on Amy. Turns out we feel the same in most instances on how to raise children. He has two kids of his own, both teenagers, and uses common sense and logic in rearing them. I'm sure he'll do the same with Amy when she spends time with him. This dinner together relieved my mind about the kind of man my daughter would be exposed to in a family situation.

4.
HANDLE PROBLEMS YOURSELF
IF YOU CAN.

Even though my husband's two daughters, who are eighteen and nineteen, don't live with us, I wanted to let them know I loved them and was concerned for their safety. I got them both car phones and agreed to pay the monthly service charges if they would pay for the calls. This arrangement worked fine for the first six months until Julie, the oldest girl, ran up a phone bill of one hundred dollars and didn't pay it on time.

I called her, and she explained that she'd just lost her job but would pay me as soon as she could. Another month went by without a payment but with an additional bill of nearly four hundred dollars. I called her again.

Since it was my gift to her, and our relationship I needed to foster, I didn't involve her father in the dilemma. Although she apologized for not paying and promised to do so as soon as she could, I told her being sorry wasn't good enough. "I cannot pay this bill myself without borrowing the money," I continued. "That's how tight our budget is. Can you at least pay fifty dollars a month on it? If not, I'll have to discontinue the phone."

She appreciated my willingness to help her, and by the next month, the first installment of fifty dollars was received. This problem helped us take another step toward establishing a good relationship.

5.
FACE IT:
YOU MAY NEVER WIN HIM OVER.

Twenty-five years after I married his father, I heard my thirty-nine-year-old stepson say, "What right did you have to come into our lives and change everything? We had a life of our own. We didn't want to live yours. You had no right to tell us what to do."

Twenty-five years of doing all I could to be a good stepmother, bridging the rocky relationship between this boy and his father, keeping the family talking. Twenty-five years of loving him, praying for him, giving him a stable home life where he had all he needed and then some.

I can't stop hearing the words in my mind: "What right did you have? . . ."

6.
IF YOU CAN'T SAY SOMETHING NICE...

The hardest thing about being a stepparent is *not* saying anything negative about the real mother, particularly when there's a long list of comments you could (and would *love* to) make. It only hurts the child when you put down her mother, and such comments make you look ridiculous. Focus on the fact that, eventually, your stepchild will become an adult and her adult, eyes will not be blinded to that parent's flaws. You'll be glad you held your tongue when your youngster praises you for being unbiased and nonjudgmental.

7.
YOUR CHILDREN NEED PEACE.

I thought my new husband wanted a good relationship with my sons when I married again. Instead, he's argumentative most of the time. He tries so hard to establish himself as the head of the house that he bullies me as well as the boys. I can't convince him that the boys are not a threat to his and my relationship, that I love him deeply even though I've loved the boys longer.

My boys try to get along with their new dad, but they can never please him. Neither can I. We're still together, but it's tough going.

My children want peace in their family. So do I.

8.
LET HIS FATHER
EXPLAIN SEX TO HIM.

As Charley's stepfather, I will certainly answer any questions about sex if he raises them, but I prefer to let his natural father do the job. That's something a father and son should share.

9.
BUILD UP YOUR
STEPCHILD'S FATHER.

My stepson Neil credits me with bringing his father back into his life. Before Ted and I married, Ted was a carefree bachelor who spent little time with his son, even though he lived on the other side of town. Now that we're married, Ted has become a Christian, and we have Neil at our house every other weekend.

The first time Neil said to me, "If it weren't for you, I wouldn't be able to see my dad," I cringed. I assured him, "Neil, that's not true. You know your dad loves to be with you."

He looked at me with sad eyes and said, "I'm entitled to my opinion."

"Yes, you are," I agreed, "but your dad's life has

changed, and he very much wants you to be a major part of it."

Even though it's natural for a stepparent to crave acceptance by a stepchild, it's important to foster respect in the child for his natural parent.

10.
IF IT'S TOO HARD TAKING TWO OR THREE STEPCHILDREN AT A TIME FOR A VISIT, HAVE ONLY ONE COME.

When my husband's three daughters visit us together, the result is pandemonium. Since they're all vying for their father's attention, verbal skirmishes result, causing tension. Then I discovered the tactic of taking the girls one at a time, and the weekends have become peaceful and fun. Brent and I are careful to give each girl the same amount of time with us. Now we thoroughly enjoy their visits, and we're getting to know them better as they grow up.

11.

ENCOURAGE STEPCHILDREN FROM DIFFERENT FAMILIES TO KNOW EACH OTHER.

My husband has been married twice before and has children by both women. The two older girls are sisters; the younger girl is an only child. I like to have all three girls visit us at once because I want them, especially the younger one, Samantha, to know she has sisters and to get along with them. Three marriages and three separate households have taken a toll on the girls, and I want to do my best to create an entire family now.

12.

KNOW THE DIFFERENCE BETWEEN A STEPFATHER AND A FATHER.

While I love my stepson very much and we have a close relationship, I never try to be more to him than his own father, who is a good man. I'm the stepfather. I won't compete with his natural father for Jared's affection and respect or strive to replace that man. I don't make Jared call me Dad for that very reason. He has one dad, and that's not me. I have to be mature enough to accept that.

13.
Let Your Stepchild Know You Like Him.

My stepson's father died when he was three. When Anthony was seven, his mother and I married. It didn't take long to see that he wanted a daddy more than anything. He clung to me when he should have been with his friends. The reason? "He's afraid you might not like him," my wife told me. "He thinks if you don't like him, you'll go away."

I had a serious talk with Anthony and assured him that not only did I love him very much, but I liked him, as well. I went on to tell him exactly why I liked him, why I thought he was a great kid, and why I was proud and happy to be his stepdad. This talk greatly relieved his mind.

14.
If You're the Natural Parent, Support Your Spouse

My husband's father set a good example for him: Even though the children are important, his wife comes before them. And even though I'm his children's stepmother, he supports me in front of them and gives me respect and love. He doesn't undermine my authority with them.

15.
SHOW THEM YOU LOVE THEM; DON'T JUST SAY IT.

I wanted my stepsons—who live several states away with their mother—to know me and to know I loved them. My solution? I arranged for John and me to have an (800) number. I told the boys, "Whenever you want to talk with your father or me, just call. Any time." I also gave them my beeper number at work, and they've used both numbers to call.

I wanted to be the one who gave the children this gift since I wanted them to know I was comfortable with, and happy that they would stay in close touch with their father. Yes, we're a little poorer financially because of this arrangement, but "our" children know they are loved and that we are always delighted, even eager, to hear from them.

16.
DON'T BE JEALOUS OF THE FORMER SPOUSE.

Even though I get along well with my wife's two daughters, lately I had to face the demon of jealousy. The girls started bringing up in their conversations times when Monica and their father, Brad, did things together. "Dad says you used to go horseback riding

every week and took us with you when we were little,"
they'd say. At first I took it to be a nostalgia trip that
shut me out by bringing up memories of when the four
of them were a family.

My wife is a wise woman who soon noticed my dis-
comfiture. "Don't be jealous of what the girls say," she
said. "They're trying to build a sense of their father and
mother together. It's like the pieces of a puzzle. You
and I are part of the puzzle and have pieces, but some
of the pieces of their dad are missing."

This kind of questioning continued for a few
months with the girls, then stopped. Taking my wife's
advice, I tried not to be jealous, and I listened carefully
to what the girls said and how they said it. I felt no sen-
timent in their words or attitude that suggested they
wanted their father in their lives more than me.

One day the questions ceased, and my wife simply
said, "They have enough of the puzzle for now."

I'm glad jealousy didn't make me resentful of either
her or the girls.

17.
LET GO OF THE HURT.

At my nineteen-year-old daughter's wedding, I
walked her down the aisle even though her mother
and I are divorced, and Ainsley has a new stepfather.
But I was hurt that my name did not appear on the
wedding invitation. When the minister asked, "Who

giveth this woman in marriage?" her mother and step-father were the ones to say, "We do." I had not been asked to join them.

Still, I came out better than my friend who had been stepfather to a girl from the time she was twelve. At the wedding of his daughter he was with the girl's mother, to whom he'd been married for eighteen years, but was given no part in the ceremony at all. The girl's natural father, who had walked out on his family when his two children were small, escorted her down the aisle.

It's best to find a way around these slights and go on with your relationships. Holding grudges solves nothing.

18.
INCLUDE VISITING STEPCHILDREN IN REGULAR PLANS

My stepdaughter, Amy, told me the other day, much to my surprise, "I love coming to visit you and Dad because you don't treat me like a guest. I feel like a member of the family." I wasn't sure what she meant at the time. Awhile later, we told her we were going to pick up some rosebushes at a nursery in a town fifteen miles away. When I asked her if she wanted to go along, she said with excitement, "Sure. Whatever you guys are gonna do, that's what I want to do, too."

19.
DON'T TALK ABOUT
ONE CHILD TO ANOTHER.

In a moment of guy-to-guy sharing, I discussed with my oldest teenage stepson, Shawn, something his younger brother had done that really bothered me. Instead of this confidence making Shawn feel as though he and I were at a mature stage of sharing, he took it as an act of disloyalty to his brother and pulled back from me. I haven't gotten him back yet.

20.
LET STEPCHILDREN KNOW
YOU'RE NOT MADE OF MONEY.

Sometimes my husband shares too much of our financial situation with his three daughters who live with their mother but visit us often. He explained to me that he does this "so they won't think we're an open pocketbook, able to spend money on them we don't have just to make them like us more." I can't fault that reasoning.

21.
DON'T LET THERE BE A DIFFERENCE BETWEEN THE PARENT AND THE STEPPARENT.

I'm in an unfortunate situation. My wife has a son by a previous marriage, and she makes it clear to me and the boy that I am only the stepfather while she is the parent and the final authority on every matter that concerns Chad. I love my stepson, but it is hard to foster a meaningful and respectful relationship with him when he is taught to regard me as little more than the man to whom his mother is married.

22.
HELP CHILDREN NAME THEIR PARENTS.

My daughter has two fathers—one, her biological father, and the other, the stepfather who raised her from the time she was two. When she was little and would visit her natural father, she didn't know what to call him because she called her stepfather Daddy. But on her own she came up with this wonderful solution: She has a Daddy Mark, her stepfather, and a Daddy Scott, her biological father. Now, in conversation, there's no doubting about whom she is speaking.

23.
LET STEPCHILD KEEP TO ROUTINE.

When Rob and I married, he brought with him his five-year-old daughter Susan. Knowing the biggest adjustment would be for her, I insisted Rob and Susan continue any special routine they had shared in the past. So, Rob went on hearing her prayers and tucking her in bed at night. He read her favorite stories and made her peanut butter sandwiches just the way she liked them. I made sure they had plenty of father/daughter time together.

Eventually, when she came to realize that I was not going to steal her daddy from her, our new family blended. Now I also read the stories, listen to her prayers, and tuck her in—and I'm not a threat but part of the family.

Peer Pressure

*Go from the presence of a foolish man,
when you do not perceive in him the lips of
knowledge.*

Proverbs 14:7

"Ken," I called out to my husband who was putting oil in the car in our garage. "Where did those bicycles come from?" I pointed up to the rafters, to three bikes I knew didn't belong to us.

Ken walked underneath them and squinted upward. "Beats me. Terry!" He then called out to our oldest son who was just now coming into the garage from the house. "Whose bikes are those?"

"Uh. . .well. . ."

"Yes?" Ken prodded him.

"I thought it would be okay to store them there."

"Whose are they?"

"My friend, Tony's."

"He has three bicycles?" I asked.

Terry took off his baseball cap and twisted it around in his hands. He couldn't look his dad or me in the eye. "I'm just keeping the bikes for Tony until he. . ." he mumbled almost incoherently.

"What?" Ken inserted.

"Takes them back."

Ken frowned. "Back to where?" he asked.

"I'm not sure."

"Ter-r-r-r-ry. . ."

Terry took a deep breath and the words rushed out of his mouth. "He stole them. From the miniature golf place on Valley View."

"*Stole them?* Terry, did you—?"

"No, Dad, I didn't steal them. I had nothing to do with it. I wasn't even there. Tony did it as a prank this morning, but now he wants to take them back, tonight, when it's dark, before he gets caught. I didn't want to store them for him. I knew you'd catch me. But he talked me into it because his garage is too small, and his folks would have seen them, and it's only for a few hours."

Ken nodded his understanding. He moved up to his tall son and put his nose to within inches of Terry's. "Terry, I'm taking the car to get some gas. When I drive back into this garage, those bikes had better be gone, or I'm taking you and Tony to the police station."

"Yes, Sir." Terry almost saluted. His dad, who had been in the navy, was one tough firefighter. He took no guff.

"I don't want a son of mine accused of stealing," Ken said.

"No, Sir."

"I'll be back in fifteen minutes. I know where the police station is."

The bikes disappeared before Ken, in the car, reached the end of the block. I had never seen Terry move so fast.

1.
ACCEPT YOURSELF AS
THE ONE WHOM GOD MADE.

We encourage Melissa to accept herself as the one whom God made and not to let other kids her age pressure her into being what she's not. Easier said than done. It's hard for teens to be themselves, or individuals, since they want to be like everyone else. They want to fit into the world's mold. They don't want to be different. "But it's the different people," I encourage her, "who make the world a better place. Dare to be different—if you're doing worthwhile things for yourself and others."

2.
PEER PRESSURE
CAN BE GOOD.

Our son wanted nothing to do with church until a new family moved in next door. There was a boy Chad's age, and they became fast friends. This boy, Rick, was involved in a youth group at his church, and he invited Chad to go to a meeting. Chad resisted at first, but because he wanted to please his friend, he finally agreed to attend. What a difference that youth group has made in our son's life! Today he's a strong Christian—because of the positive peer pressure of a fine friend.

3.
WARN YOUR CHILD OF
THE CONSEQUENCES OF BEING GOOD.

Because Amy was homeschooled for most of her life, she didn't have as much peer pressure as some of her church friends who went to public school. In Amy's second year of high school, though, I had to go to work, and Amy was forced to attend public school. Before sending her off, I talked with her at length about the pressures she would face from kids who didn't understand her commitment to the Lord. They might want her to do things she was not raised to do.

"There's nothing wrong with you, Sweetheart, when you're rejected by some kids. If they don't like you for who you are, then they're not the kind of friends who will be good for you."

Amy had some rough moments over the next few years, but her father and I and our church kept affirming the thought that it's okay to be good, to love God, to want to serve Him. "You're not weird; you're blessed," we told her.

Amy conquered peer pressure by believing in her own self-worth.

4.
LEARN WHAT PEER PRESSURE REALLY IS.

We believe peer pressure is not just a social problem but an emotional and spiritual one, as well. We watch Adam's personality vigilantly and look for signs that he might be struggling with self-worth and his relationship with God. These situations we deal with at home as best we can and hope we catch them in time before they spill over into his wanting to please his friends more than his parents and God.

5.
DON'T TELL YOUR KIDS YOU UNDERSTAND WHAT THEY'RE GOING THROUGH.

I have said, "I know what you're going through," once too often to Brittany, especially at a time when she was having a problem at school with some of her friends.

"You don't know at all what I'm going through, Dad," she lashed out at me. "You don't know what it's like to be a teenager nowadays. It's different from when you were in school. There's more pressure now."

Every generation feels they're going through the toughest time. A parent needs to be sensitive to his child's struggle.

6.
INVEST YOUR TIME IN YOUR TEEN.

I've learned from past experience that I need to spend a lot of time with my teenage daughters, even though they think they can take care of themselves. Mike and I learned the hard way that the people our teens are around the most have the greatest influence on them, no matter how well we have raised them.

When my oldest daughter was drifting away from us, I realized, after many sleepless nights spent in prayer, that we needed to find something we could do together as a family. For us, the activity became karate, but it can be anything you learn and work on regularly as a family unit. If it's something physical, something that makes you sweat for thirty minutes or more, you'll be adding to your family's good health and reducing their stress levels.

Parenting is a full-time job from which you never retire, and just when you think you've got it figured out, it changes. Being the primary influence in your children's lives is good for them and makes you feel good about your parenting skills.

7.
KIDS THINK THEY'RE INVINCIBLE, BECAUSE THEIR FRIENDS THINK THEY'RE INVINCIBLE.

Kids are so used to instant gratification that they don't grasp that what they're doing today has a profound effect on the rest of their lives. They see themselves and their friends as invincible; they're sure they can have everything they want, one way or another.

When I try to talk to my son about the consequences of his actions, he laughs and says, "Dad, you're not cool. My buddies and I have life all figured out."

I wish I did.

8.
CHURCH FRIENDS CAN ENCOURAGE QUESTIONABLE BEHAVIOR.

Nearly every teenager in our church was allowed to see a wildly popular movie that was rated PG-13. Naturally, our two sons wanted to see it, too. But we made a decision some years back, as an entire family, Mom and Dad, too, not to see PG-13 movies because of the expected violence, nudity, and profanity.

In a review in a national Christian magazine to which we subscribe, this movie was not recommended. Adults we questioned who had seen the film told us of the nudity in the picture, vulgar language, and the glorification of sex between unmarried young people. Later, when we discussed the film with our children, our sons surprised us by agreeing not to see it, saying they understood the reasons why we and so many Christians were against it.

We didn't go to it, either. Just because we're adults doesn't mean we should put all these immoral images into our heads and hearts any more than our children should.

9.
Acceptance by Peers Versus Acceptance by Society Is a Difficult Struggle.

When my daughter came to the supper table wearing black nail polish, my husband nearly choked on his food. "I know you hate it," Leslie said, "but my friends love it and think it's cool."

I said, calmly, "There's nothing intrinsically wrong with wearing black nail polish, Sweetheart, or having your nose or lip pierced or your hair shaved in a mohawk and dyed purple, but society makes judgments based on what is seen. You have a decision to make. Either you avoid the things society views as bizarre, or you deal with a society that thinks you are bizarre. Yes, it's insignificant if you wear black nail polish, but don't be surprised when an employer won't hire you. These are the consequences, and the choice is yours."

I held my breath.

"I think I'll take the polish off," Leslie said. "I really need that job at the restaurant."

10.
"I Can Be My Own Person."

My seventeen year-old daughter told me she used to feel the only way she could "fit in" with her school friends was to be like everyone else, wear the same clothes, and have the same opinions. She wanted to be accepted, respected, and involved.

After joining a local church youth group, however, she said, "I can be my own person at church. They accept me for who I am and respect my point of view. They want me to join in the activities, and I don't have to be anyone but myself."

Even though she still likes to "fit in" with the school crowd, she no longer feels compelled to do so.

11.
"Everybody's Watching It."

Unlike some of their friends, who have their own television sets in their bedrooms, our teenage daughters have to watch TV on our one television in the family room. We watch little commercial television and have never allowed our children unrestricted access to watch whatever they wish.

A few months ago, our daughters came to us and asked to watch a show all their friends were talking about. In fact, the show was so popular that its most recent episode was the main topic at school every Wednesday. We agreed to let them watch one episode under certain conditions: We would watch it with them, and afterward they would listen to our views as well as express their own opinions regarding its content. However, we would have the sole and final judgment over whether they could continue to watch the show on a regular basis.

They agreed, and we watched it and found it suitable. Each week we watch it as an older family group (the younger kids are in bed). It provides a good vehicle for discussing issues that might not come up otherwise.

12.
LET THEIR BEHAVIOR DICTATE YOUR LENIENCY.

While I (usually) let my kids wear goofy clothes and hairdos, and they *think* they are "following the crowd," there are conditions to my tolerance. Just as there are certain absolute no-nos (drinking, drugs, driving fast, cursing, and so on), there are plenty of areas of leeway, too. Their behavior dictates what I allow and what I won't.

For example, if I let them wear plaid flannel shirts over white tee-shirts to school (ick!) and some area of their behavior starts to deteriorate, I pull back on the tolerance level and we do a closet clean-up and dress the part of what I consider to be "a good kid." When I give in on an atrocious hairstyle and then their grades drop, they have to find a new, mother-approved look. Doesn't take my smart sons long to clean up the offending areas of their lives if they want the privileges of looking like the peers they admire.

13.
MAKE THE RULES CLEAR.

When our two sons told us they were thinking of getting their ears and noses pierced, my husband made clear our position: "If you ever come home with anything pierced, you have two options: (1) Remove the pierced earring yourself, or (2) I'll remove it for you."

14.
CHURCH YOUTH GROUPS HOLD KIDS TO CHRIST.

Our oldest son went all through high school being involved in a youth group. Most of the friends he hung out with were also in the group. He never got into trouble or rebelled against us or going to church.

When our twins got into junior high, we lost our youth group. This is a crucial age for kids, an age when they need all the support they can get. At their school, alcohol use was high, with about 70 percent of the students drinking socially. I had always thought a strong family made a difference in kids' lives, but our twins began to flounder and got involved with the wrong crowd.

When our youngest son became a teen, he had a youth group but didn't want to get involved. He began to argue with us and rebel against going to church. As an answer to prayer, last summer, while on a church

campout, he connected with some of the other teens.
Since then I never have to tell him he has to go to
church. He's there when I'm not there.

I have heard some parents say, "Church doesn't
mean anything to my child; he just goes to be with his
friends," as though that's bad. Wanting to be with
Christian friends is a positive thing. When my sons are
in an organized church group, they have a chance to
go in the right direction.

15.
A Signed Contract Eases Peer Pressure.

When our children were younger, we had family
conferences, usually around the dinner table, where
we talked over what kind of family we were and the
rules we wanted to live by. When the oldest son and
daughter reached their teen years, we decided to draw
up a contract of behavior with them, worked out ami-
cably (most of the time) between us. Signatures were
required. Punishment of some kind was the result of
breaking the contract.

By deciding on a contract of behavior before problems arise, our children know exactly what is expected
of them. It helps them deal with peer pressure when
friends want them to stay out later than they are
allowed or go places we won't let them go. It saves their
"face" while putting the responsibility on the parents,
which is fine with us.

Here are a few of the points in the contract (written from the child's point of view):

(1) I can only stay out two weeknights until 10 p.m., unless I am involved in sports or church activities. Other nights I must spend at home.

(2) My curfew for Friday and Saturday nights is 11:30.

(3) Every boy/girl I date must be brought inside to meet my parents before we leave for the date and again afterward.

(4) I will not be involved with drinking or drugs.

(5) My curfew cannot be broken without calling home for permission to do so—and then, I shouldn't count on it.

(6) I know that if any problem develops with this contract, discussion will be held to see if changes are warranted.

16.
It Only Takes One Bad Friend.

Our oldest son hung out with the right friends, and they never pressured him to do bad things. The next two boys got involved with the wrong kids and ended up getting into trouble. Not only did they make wrong choices, but they looked at us, their parents, as though we were from Mars. There is a powerful pull away from family ties if your children are with the wrong people. Peer pressure can destroy family values.

Our youngest child is like an only child since her

siblings are so much older. I see her friends as an important asset, and I pray for her to make the right choices in friends. So far she has, with God's help.

17.
CHURCH CAN LOSE OUT TO FRIENDS.

When we moved to a new neighborhood, we took too long in finding a church home. Our son formed questionable friendships and got involved in unhealthy peer activities, so that when we finally did settle on a dynamic, Bible-preaching church, Jedd didn't want to take time away from his own pursuits to attend with us.

"No, I'm not going!" he announced. "I just want to stay home and go on the Internet."

Even when we told him this church had a strong, active youth group, he was resistant. "Maybe next week," he said. This became a ritual saying, week after week.

Finally we said, "Jedd, we're going. Attending church is more important than your computer or hanging out with your friends at the mall."

It took a few weeks of not backing down and practically dragging Jedd out of the house Wednesday nights and Sunday mornings, but finally we heard the words we'd been waiting for: "The church's youth group is great, Dad. Our adviser really understands kids my age."

Jedd's involvement with the church didn't keep him from making mistakes in the future, but his Christian friends and the church staff, and the God-given morals we gave him that they reinforced, were the major guiding forces for him when he needed them.

18.
GIVING IN TO PEER PRESSURE WHEN IT COMES TO CLOTHES DOESN'T BOTHER ME.

I refuse to argue with Ashley over clothes. She has so few ways to express her individuality, and besides, what's a big deal with her today won't be tomorrow. As she is growing, the outfit I hate today probably won't fit her in three months. Besides, her tastes change almost daily.

As long as her clothes meet my standard of modesty, and I can afford them, I let her pick what she wants.

19.
APPEAL TO YOUR CHILD'S INTELLIGENCE.

Kids are smarter than we sometimes think. Give them your reasons for not liking certain clothes—logical ones—and you'll be surprised at their grasp of those truths.

When tight, short clothes started being popular with my daughter's group of friends, all I said was, "Go ahead and wear those things, but keep one thing in mind: If you catch a guy with meat, you'll get a dog every time." That thought worked for her; it made sense. I have even heard her repeat it to some of her friends.

20.
THERE'S STRENGTH WHEN FRIENDS STICK TOGETHER.

Both my sons carry cards in their wallets bearing their signatures saying they will wait until marriage to have sex. Most of their friends have this same viewpoint. It was introduced in their youth group at church. This kind of peer support helps the boys to honor their vows and makes us, as their parents, proud of them.

21.
PEERS CAN INSPIRE GOOD HABITS
WHEN PARENTS CAN'T.

The most challenging aspect of "teenagehood" has been getting Harry to take his schoolwork seriously. He's bright but alas, often unmotivated. I have been unsuccessful in getting him to buckle down, and the threat of summer school, grounding, and so on has not worked.

Fortunately, Harry's school system is pretty good, and I have learned to depend on their resources. I would strongly urge parents to find out what programs are available in their child's school and make use of what they have to offer.

Harry now reports to a teaching assistant in the math and sciences department every morning, who checks to make sure he has completed all his homework assignments (he does not check content). Harry responds well to this approach and likes knowing that someone, other than his mother, is watching out for him.

Tutoring is usually available from National Honor Society students in any subject and is free of charge. This has also worked well for Harry, and he believes his peers, more readily than me at this point, when they tell him the importance of good grades.

RESPECT

Furthermore, we have had human fathers who corrected us, and we paid them respect. Shall we not much more readily be in subjection to the Father of spirits and live?

HEBREWS 12:9

I didn't mean to overhear the conversation between Lisa and her girlfriend, Kristine, but I did.

Kristine said, "We have to go to my grandma's tomorrow night for her birthday. I *hate* going to these parties. They're so boring."

"I like our family get-togethers," Lisa said. "My grand parents are there, and my uncle, and my aunt and her five kids, and us."

"Yuck!"

"No, really, it can be fun. How old is your grandmother?"

"Ancient, seventy-something."

"My grandma's seventy-five, and she's still so pretty. She sings and plays the piano and is funny. I like to hear her tell stories about growing up in Chicago. She was born in England, but her family moved to the United States when she was six. 'I had heard, before we got here,' she says, 'there were gangsters on every street corner. I was scared to come to America.'"

While the conversation between the girls went on to other topics, I was proud of my daughter for having such respect for her grandmother that she would share this with a friend. Not only was she willing to listen to Dorothy Alice Roberts Peterson tell stories from the "old days," but she enjoyed them!

Someday when I am ancient—in my seventies—I hope someone will respect me enough to listen to the stories I can tell. And will I ever have stories to tell.

1.
RESPECT COMES THE OLD-FASHIONED WAY: IT HAS TO BE EARNED.

As parents, we realize we cannot demand respect from our daughter—it has to be earned. And it is earned by developing a level of trust. We need to respect her private world, as well, but be ready for any "open window" or vulnerable moment when she will let us in. We take advantage of that moment and listen to her without rebuke or demands. We try to comfort, encourage, and share our own experiences of imperfection. We know this will build a trusting and respectful relationship between us.

2.
BEING A PAL CAN MEAN A LOSS OF RESPECT.

Teenagers don't need another pal, but they do need a parent. I made the mistake of trying to be my son's buddy when he was between thirteen and fourteen. Then when I had to be a father, he didn't like it at all and gave me a lot of flack. I lost his respect for awhile until I gave up being his pal and concentrated, instead, on being the best dad I could be.

3.
NEVER ALLOW DISRESPECT.

One behavior that particularly bothers my wife and me is when our daughter talks back. Immediately, I place my hand across her mouth and say, "That kind of talk will not be tolerated. If I allow disrespect, as your authority, someday you may disrespect God, and this will be to your detriment. I love you too much to let that happen."

My daughter tries to assure me that will never happen, but I remain unconvinced.

4.
HERE'S HOW TO GET RID OF SASSINESS.

"How do we get rid of your mouthiness?" I asked Sarah one day. With straightforward honesty she said, "Take away a privilege, Mom, like a babysitting job. When you take my money, you are really punishing me. I'll think twice before mouthing off to you again." When I gave her an Oh, yeah? look, she laughed and said, "Trust me, Mom."

5.
RESPECT GOES BOTH WAYS IN A FAMILY.

"You're always complaining that I don't respect you, Dad," my son Chad challenged me one day. "How about you respecting me, too? How often do you take me at my word? I get the feeling you don't trust me. You don't respect me. How do you think that makes me feel?"

6.
RESPECT STARTS WITH GOD.

I once told Jason, "The Holy Spirit lives in you just as He does in me, and He can lead you to make decisions and wise choices. Respect His wisdom and listen to Him, and you won't go wrong."

We don't give Jason a list of things he can do and things he can't. Instead we give guidelines and let him make decisions based on those parameters. It's like playing football. We tell him: "As long as you stay on the field and follow the guidelines, you'll have the freedom to play the game. However, we, as coach and referee, are always nearby to call the plays, if necessary, or to blow the whistle if there's a foul, or to give advice, especially if asked."

Jason understands that analogy, and he is pretty trustworthy.

7.
IT'S A SIGN OF RESPECT WHEN THEY STAY HOME.

Sometimes I get tired of seeing the same friend over for dinner, most of the time unannounced. But then I remind myself that home is the best place for my kids, and it's better this way than not knowing whom they're with or where they are. I take it as a sign of respect that they invite their friends to our home—and appreciate my cooking.

8.
CHILDREN NEED TO RESPECT THEIR PARENTS.

In those moments when our daughter Maryann is adamantly opposing us and showing no respect for our authority, we remind her of the following: (1) We love you and want what is best for you; (2) You need to pray about the situation and seek what God would have you to do; and (3) We are your parents, and God has put us in authority over you to protect and guide you. Therefore, you need to obey God by obeying us.

She may pout for awhile, but in the end she respects us for our stand, realizing it was done for her good.

9.
PLAY FAIR.

When your child shows disrespect for you or some authority figure, don't use the words "always" and "never" in describing how they act (example: "You always use that tone of voice. . ."). Don't point out how one of their friends is more respectful (polite, well-mannered, more cooperative) than they are. Such an approach only builds resentment and is not fair.

10.
SHOULD WORK TAKE PRECEDENCE OVER CHURCH?

When our teenage son applied for his first job, I urged him to say this to the grocery store manager: "I cannot work Sundays or Wednesday evenings. Those times are reserved for church. But I will work any other time that you require."

My son didn't believe he could do that and still get a job, but he respected my request. The manager admired his honesty and the fact that James presented himself as a decent kid who could be trusted because he had values. He got the job and every one he's applied for since. And he never works Sundays or Wednesdays.

11.
YOUR CLOTHES ARE ONE WAY
PEOPLE JUDGE YOU.

Being middle-aged and middle-class parents, we find the hip-hop and frumpy-style clothing not at all appealing. I remember, though, in my hippie days, my parents were equally upset with my sense of style. I promised myself then that I would never hinder my children's style of dress. Today, I'm rethinking that vow.

While our first son always dresses in conservative jeans and button-down shirts, our youngest teenage son, Brandon, has a different outlook altogether. He isn't bothered by our dismay at his sloppy appearance.

At a professional hockey game, I started my own game with him to see if he could guess the profession or lifestyle of other spectators by observing the way they were dressed. It was fun to glance at someone and try to guess who was a doctor, lawyer, sanitation engineer, teacher, truck driver, mechanic, and so forth. We also shared how we would interact with that person. Did he appear trustworthy, shady, or just plain unsavory? Would we respect her opinion?

"When people see you dressed as you are, what do you think is their first reaction?" I asked Brandon. "Do they trust you? Think you are intelligent? Worry that you'll spread some disease? Is their assessment accurate or justified?"

Brandon finally realized the connection between his appearance and how others viewed him. Whether wearing certain kinds of clothes was right or wrong wasn't the issue; it was a case of first impressions often making a major difference in a relationship.

That night Brandon learned that appearance often determines how a person initially reacts to you and that you should dress in a manner consistent with how you wish to be perceived.

12.
No Blue Jeans on Sunday Nights.

Many kids at our church have started wearing blue jeans to church Sunday nights. When Andrea gets upset with me about my rule of no jeans, I explain that God's house is not the local carwash. I feel it's a sign of disrespect to Him to wear our grubbiest clothes to His place of worship. I know God doesn't look on the outer appearance, but dressing sloppily to go to church shows me an irreverent attitude.

I tell Andrea, "I know some of your friends may disagree with me, but this is my belief and that of some other people my age—people we love. I don't want to offend them by the way I dress. There are plenty of other places and times when you can wear jeans to your heart's content."

13.
Running Laps for Bad Behavior Works.

We struggled with how to discipline our boys when they reached their teen years. Spankings were inappropriate and ineffective and room isolation was a waste of time, although we still use that method to diffuse overheated conversations.

Consequently, we developed more creative acts of discipline. For lapses in manners and respect for others, our sons do push-ups and sit-ups. When they treat parents or one another poorly, they have to run laps.

This form of punishment is particularly effective if they have to do it just when they want to be doing something else. It focuses their attention on their improper behavior and the consequences that can be inconvenient as well as difficult.

14.
Choose Your Nos.

The best advice on parenting I've had was from my mother. She said, "If there's not a reason to say no, then say yes. If you say no all the time, the child stops respecting you as a parent who can make sound judgments."

15.
Respect Is a Large Part of Discipline.

When children become teenagers, we parents must respect their abilities to make their own decisions and be responsible for their own actions. No sink or swim stuff, though. Cliff and I are finding parenting teens to be quite a balancing act. We monitor their decisions closely and offer advice and help, as they will accept it. We do our best to give them an environment in which they can succeed by being supportive, involved, and in touch with what they are doing and with whom they are interacting.

It's not easy letting your teenagers start flying from the nest, but we want them to know we believe they can do it successfully. As much as possible, we respect their efforts.

16.
IF YOU HAVE YOUR CHILD'S RESPECT, HE'LL LISTEN TO YOU.

There is one friend of Johnny's who comes across as the nicest, friendliest kid, but I've found out from a reliable source (an adult) that he's really a snake in the grass. I've asked Johnny not to see him or bring him to our home.

Of course, I can't monitor what Johnny's doing every second of the day when he's not home. He's seventeen and has his own car. If he chooses to sneak behind my back and see this boy, he can do that.

It goes back to respect—his respect for our judgment—that we've nurtured in him from birth. Johnny respects his mother and me, and, although I'm not saying he's never done something he shouldn't, he hears us when we speak, understands our position, and obeys, as far as we know.

17.
ENCOURAGE YOUR CHILDREN TO RESPECT
THE RULES OF YOUR HOUSE.

They're all gonna do it. . .bring home a friend who turns your stomach with his dirty hands, grimy baseball cap, or crude behavior. Our sons know that in our home we're the ones who set behavior standards, and we expect them to respect that. If their friends don't want to wash their hands before they eat with us, or remove their filthy cap, or stop using language we find offensive, then they don't belong here. We never embarrass these less-than-pleasant friends; we expect John and Tracy to let them know the rules of the house.

18.
NEVER STOP TRYING TO INSTILL GOOD MANNERS.

Having good manners is a sign of respect for others and is something that takes time to teach. At every age kids need to learn something else. We started by teaching Bryan how to hold his fork properly, why it's important not to slurp his soup, and the value of placing a napkin on his lap. Telephone etiquette took awhile to master, but he finally got the hang of asking, "May I take a message?" Then came getting him to write the said message legibly so we could read it later.

Now that's he's a teenager, I'm working on language, in particular, trying to keep him from saying "yeah" instead of "yes." I have him hold the chair out for me when we sit down to dinner and open the door for me when we go into a building. He addresses adults respectfully as "sir" and "ma'am."

Manners and showing respect are so important to us that we reward Bryan when he is courteous. We pay for him to play miniature golf with his friends, help him buy some special piece of clothing, or let him stay up later than usual when a friend is over.

RESPONSIBILITY

If anyone will not work, neither shall he eat.
2 THESSALONIANS 3:10

"Dad, I need a car, and there's one for sale at the lot on Chapman. The owner said I could have it for—"

My eyebrows shot up at the same time Ken held up his hand to keep our seventeen-year-old son, Terry, from going any further. "You need a car?"

"Just for running around."

"Running around costs money."

"I'll get a job to pay for it."

Ken smiled. I smiled. We said at the same time, "A job?" It was our fondest dream come true.

"Sure, I'll get a job to pay for the car," Terry assured us with all his charm on display. "But I need the car first, so I can look for the job."

Ken's smile disappeared. "There are a dozen fast-food places within walking distance of our house," he told Terry.

"I know, Dad, but I want a more substantial job." He straightened his shoulders.

I could tell he was sincere, and I was glad the possibility of owning a car was providing the necessary incentive. Terry had not been anxious to get a job before.

"One of the firemen at work has a Volkswagen for sale," Ken told Terry. "I'll look into it."

Two days later there was an eight-year-old "Bug" sitting in the driveway. Terry was ecstatic.

"I expect to be paid back the nine hundred dollars I paid for this car, Terry," Ken told him firmly.

"Sure. No problem, Dad. I'll start looking for that job right away."

A week passed. Two weeks. Three weeks. Terry drove his car everywhere but didn't find a job. Ken suspected he wasn't trying all that hard.

"Terry, you have one month to find a job and start paying off that car. Otherwise I'm selling it."

"Sure, Dad."

One month passed. Terry did not have a job. Ken sold the car.

If there was one thing our children knew for a certainty about their dad, it was that he was a man of his word. If he promised to do something, he'd do it. Likewise, if one of his children promised to do something, he held them responsible for that promise.

1.
KNOW WHERE YOUR CHILDREN ARE.

Richy was supposed to be home by 11 P.M. after getting off work at the gas station at 10:45. When he called at 11:20, I was relieved and angry at the same time.

"Where are you?" I asked him.

"I'm sorry, Mom. Jim, the owner, and I got to talking after the station closed, and I forgot to call you before I left."

Richy thought that explanation was good enough to excuse his being late without permission, but it wasn't. I grounded him for two weeks, much to his dismay.

"But I called," he offered in reaction to what he thought was my unjust reaction.

"The rule of the house is that you are home from your job by eleven o'clock. No excuses. It's important to be responsible, Richy, to be on time. If you don't develop this habit, you could be late for work and lose your job. You could be late to catch a plane that will take you to a neat vacation. You could be late for the birth of your child—"

"Mom, puh-leeze," he groaned, "I get the point. Be responsible. Be on time."

2.
HAVING A RESPONSIBILITY
MEANS LEARNING.

Give kids responsibility by teaching them a skill of
some kind. Show them how to do what you want them to
do. Show them again. Be patient. Don't get upset if they
don't get it right the first time, or the second, or third.
Think of yourself at work. Did you learn your job the first
day? The first week? Month?

Sometimes when a child doesn't carry through on
a responsibility, it's because he doesn't really know
how to.

Responsible behavior comes from informed decisions. I think my teenagers are sick of hearing me say,
"There are no perfect solutions to any problem; just
solutions with the least problems attached."

Our method of teaching responsibility is through
informed decisions. First, we review the situation, then
we "fact find" on each solution, evaluating the negatives
and positives. Once all avenues are explored, the decision is based not on emotion but on whichever solution
offers the best resolution with the least amount of negatives attached. Or, at worst, the solution you can live
with in spite of the negatives it creates.

3.
ONCE TEENS COMMIT TO DOING SOMETHING, THEY MUST HONOR THEIR WORD.

Once you commit to do something, we tell our teenage children, you must carry through the best you can and honor your word. Although my sons have gone through some tough situations when the promises they made went awry, they still could have avoided the consequences by lying or being deceitful. We thank the Lord that years of discipline have helped them make the right decisions. Today they are extremely well respected because of their individual honesty and good sense.

4.
DON'T BE AFRAID TO LET TEENS MAKE MISTAKES.

We had to allow Alisa to fail in order to teach her true responsibility, and then we had to have the right attitude about her failures. We didn't want her to suffer, but we realized we couldn't keep her in a box and make all her decisions for her. She had to learn on her own, and failure is the best training ground. Whether meeting the standards of our family or those of the school or an employer, we have had to let her go.

She has a paper route that requires being responsible. At times, she has failed to meet those expectations and has suffered the consequences—but she has learned from those failures.

5.

FAILURE WITH EFFORT IS ACCEPTABLE; FAILURE WITHOUT EFFORT IS NOT.

What more do I need to say?

6.

ASK KIDS WHAT THEY WANT TO DO.

"Why don't you ever ask me what responsibilities I want?" Jeremy asked us angrily. "All you ever do is make rules and give me orders, like I was a slave or something. Don't I have any rights around here? Would it be such a big deal for me to be able to say, 'I'd rather wash the dishes for a week than dust the living room'?"

7.

THINK LIKE A CHAMPION.

I often recite this "saying" to my son: "Think like a champion, work like a champion, be the champion!"

8.

LET TEENS KNOW YOU TRUST THEM BUT ARE KEEPING AN EYE ON THEM, TOO.

Since both my wife and I work full time, our son, Brad, must be on his own until we get home. "We expect you to behave responsibly," we tell him. "That means letting us know where you'll be, whom you'll be with, and what you're doing. Because we love you, Son, we need to be sure nothing happens to you. That's our responsibility."

Fortunately, Brad has responded well in the last couple of years, and we haven't had too many problems. On the few occasions that he has not held up his side of the deal, he has not been allowed for a few days to have friends over, go into town on his skateboard, or join friends at the pizza place.

9.
MAKE A CONTRACT WITH A NEW DRIVER.

Our daughter has just started to drive. Angela knows driving involves new freedoms, and we want to yoke those intoxicating freedoms with common-sense responsibilities. The result of our thinking is a writtem "contract" with specific rules for the use of the car. Areas covered include curfews, driving to work, calling if there's a problem with deadlines, where she can go, where she can't, what happens if rules are broken.

It's worked remarkably well with Angela. We're going to do the same thing when our second child begins to drive.

10.
AS YOUR TEENS GROW, SO GROW THEIR RESPONSIBILITIES.

Teens are not adults! But they are growing into them. Responsibility, then, needs to be given to them slowly, growing in scope as youngsters mature.

If they backslide, set a few limits and consequences for messing up. Tell them what you are doing: "Yes, you may go to this activity on Friday. . . . You've gotten all your homework done. . . . Your attitude has been great. . . . You've been diligent with your chores. . . . You've earned it. . . . No, you can't have your friends over. Your only job, the cleaning of the bathroom, has not been done all week. I can't reward you with the privilege of having friends over."

11.
Follow Through With Promises, Positive or Negative.

I've watched my best friend promise to take away a privilege from her daughter because of some behavior and then never make it happen. Sad to say, I've seen Kimberly smile when her mom is threatening; she suspects the threat will never materialize.

12.
Learning to Make Good Decisions Takes Practice.

Our children have been allowed to make decisions on a step-by-step format as they've grown up. When they were little, we made sure they had all the information they needed about a certain situation, then let them make small decisions based on their understanding. As they grew older and showed good judgment, we allowed them to make larger decisions.

We've never forced them to decide a certain way. If we don't agree with a decision, we point out the pitfalls or consequences. Once they make a decision, we encourage them to follow through and give it their best shot. If it doesn't work out, we assist them with redirection and support. To say "I told you so" would undermine their confidence in their decision-making abilities.

13.
TEACHING RESPONSIBILITY CAN STRENGTHEN RELATIONSHIPS.

I admit it, teaching my teenager to drive a car terrified me. The very thought of getting into the passenger seat, strapped in, while my darling son maneuvered tons of steel around first a parking lot, then city streets, left me trembling.

This harrowing experience, though, turned out to be one of the most precious of my life because Greg and I found we talked more easily with each other in the car than anywhere else. The driving lessons that began as half-hour excursions into terror (for me) turned into two-hour explorations of our town and the deepening of our father/son relationship.

Even when Greg backed into a parked police car in a parking lot, I didn't panic. He learned a lot about responsibility that day, and I learned how rewarding it is to be understanding of another's panic.

14.
APPRECIATE THE FACT THAT YOUR TEEN HAS A LIFE OF HER OWN TO LIVE.

"I wish you'd tell me ahead of time when you want me to babysit Ryan," seventeen-year-old Jessica told me the other day. "I don't mind taking care of him, but sometimes I make plans with my friends, and then you expect me to cancel them at the last minute whenever you need me. It's not fair."

She was right. I had not been respectful of her life. When I acknowledged that, she was surprised. Then I was surprised when she said, "I could be better about letting you know my plans, Mom."

Mutual respect between parent and child can solve a lot of "minidilemmas."

15.
DON'T BE TOO PROTECTIVE.

—

I was too protective of Julie. I wouldn't allow her to ride with any of her friends unless they'd had their driver's licenses for two years. I put up my own kind of "road blocks" that prevented her from getting her own license, even though she'd taken driver's ed. At seventeen, she was anxious to take on this new responsibility, and she thought I'd be happy, too, because she could then help with the tasks that required driving. Instead, I treated her like a little girl.

"How do you expect me to be a good driver if I don't have any practice?" she asked me in total frustration with my attitude.

I knew she was right. I had to let her spread her wings. I went to my purse and got out the car keys. "Let's go see about getting you a license," I told her. I'll never forget the breadth of her smile or the pure joy in her eyes. If we want our children to fly, we have to let go.

16.
DRIVING PRIVILEGES MUST BE EARNED.

For the year prior to our teenager getting his learner's permit, we insisted that he earn a 2.5 GPA or better in school. Plus, he had to get a part-time job during the summer and on weekends to pay for his share of the car insurance.

Need I say these requirements were not met by jumping through hoops of joy? Still, taking responsibility for a much-desired privilege made him a safer, more sensible driver.

No longer does my son have to hear his grandparents say, "Those kids don't appreciate what it means to work for what they get." No-sirree! Now Bob and Brent hear from Grandma and Grandpa, "Well done. We're proud of your efforts."

17.
URGING RESPONSIBILITY LEADS TO A BETTER ATTITUDE.

Gordon's uncooperative attitude pops up whenever it comes time to choose between participating in family activities or household chores and spending time with friends. I tell him, "The way you treat me (his mother) about doing these kinds of things is probably the way you'll treat your future wife about fulfilling obligations."

By acknowledging his impending adulthood and showing him I care that he has a healthy, happy relationship with his wife, I help him see that part of my "job" is to guide him toward a mature manhood.

18.
STAYING OUT LATE CALLS FOR RESPONSIBLE BEHAVIOR.

If my son wants the privilege and responsibility of staying out late, he must adhere to certain rules: (1) Stay in "safe" places. This means hanging around with friends he can trust and in places where there is adult help nearby. (2) If he's going to be thirty minutes later than he told me in getting home, I want a phone call. No excuses—the line was busy. . .no phone nearby. . .didn't have change—are accepted.

19.
FOUR WORDS WE DON'T ALLOW IN OUR HOUSE.

Our four kids have learned to never, ever, under any circumstances use the words "made me do it" prefaced by a name. Kevin made me do it. My teacher made me do it. "Since you are not a robot that must be programmed by a human being," my wife or I tell them, "you are capable of saying no to a suggestion you know is wrong."

They know, from their reading of the Bible, that not even the devil can make them do something against their will.

20.
BEING RESPONSIBLE LEADS
TO BEING SUCCESSFUL.

I know that for my kids to be successful, they have to be responsible. Besides stressing the importance of doing well in school and teaching them to care for their own belongings, I have taught them from junior high on how to care for a home and their personal needs. Someday they will be living in a dorm or an apartment during college, and I don't want them to "stress out" over "making a home" while they should be concentrating on their studies.

So, during their high school years, I've added a few extra chores. They've learned how to mop a floor, clean bathrooms, water plants, do laundry, change their beds, and cook, to name a few responsibilities.

They weren't too keen at first to be doing more work, but I explained how these skills would benefit them. "By helping me with my jobs," I told them, "I'll have more time to do fun things with you." And they have made sure I did those fun things! We've gone to water parks, hiked, biked, watched movies, and played ball.

Michael, a senior, has no worries about leaving home to go to college—except maybe money. He's ready to be out on his own. (An added benefit of being responsible is that our kids have good self-esteem.) I've concluded that the more they can do on their own, and do it well, the better they'll feel about themselves.

21.
LET THEM BE RESPONSIBLE FOR THEIR WORK CLOTHES.

As soon as my son started working in a pizza place, he began whining to me that his work clothes weren't clean. The solution? I taught him how to wash them himself. It's amazing how this simple responsibility has matured him. It's like watching a young bird learn to fly. His attitude toward me—that I should be doing everything for him—changed overnight once he grasped the simple concept that he should be responsible for himself.

22.
TEACH TEENS TO TAKE CARE
OF THEMSELVES.

I've told my sons, who are seventeen and nineteen, "It's not women's work to wash and iron clothes." When they groan about these new chores, I say, "Someday your wives will thank me." I only insist they do their own work clothes. Everyone in the family does general laundry, even my husband.

23.
MAKE A LIST OF CHORES;
LET THEM CHOOSE WHAT TO DO.

Every weekend I make out a list of chores that need to be done around the house and property and pin it to the pantry wall in the kitchen. This list may include scrub your shower, your sink, your toilet, the floor of your room, vacuum the house, clean up the kitchen, load or unload the dishwasher, mow the lawn, buy milk, get bread at the discount bakery, and so on.

While I don't assign anything to the kids, I do say, "Here's the list. Put your name beside three chores this week." My teenagers must manage their time to be sure they get the chores done. Such an approach boosts their self-esteem because they can choose what they know how to do and do well. If they don't do their share, some activity they want to do is denied.

24.
KIDS NEED TO HAVE CHOICES.

Kids have to feel they have choices. "You can do this or you can do that," I've often told our three daughters, "and here are the consequences of each." Drill it into their heads that consequences always go with choices. Two words: choices and consequences.

25.
EVERYONE WORKS FOR THE FAMILY IN OUR HOUSE.

We don't pay our teens for working around the house and yard. That's expected, because they're part of our family. Each of us works for the good of the others. However, we do reward for going above and beyond what's required. We let Greg or Cindy know their efforts are appreciated and recognized. By the same token, for work not done, there is a consequence, a privilege taken away.

Self-Esteem

*"You shall love the L*ORD* your God with all your heart, with all your soul, with all your strength, and with all your mind," and "your neighbor as yourself."*

L<small>UKE</small> 10:27

As parents, we always hope our children will look back fondly on their growing-up years. We hope they'll remember all those nights we nursed them back to health while giving up our favorite television programs, or the countless evenings we sat on a cold metal bench at the baseball field watching their team lose twenty to four, or the many times we spent way too much money at amusement parks.

Listen then to one of Lisa's most ingrained memories of her years as a teen: "Dad was always complaining on how I used my fork. I dreaded eating with you."

I frowned, not remembering a single traumatic moment when Ken demolished Lisa's self-esteem over a fork. But when I asked him about it, he remembered the situation exactly.

"Lisa used to pile huge amounts of food on her fork at one time, open her mouth wide, and shovel it in. All I said was, 'Lisa, no one will steal your food off your plate. Just take a little at a time.'"

Today Lisa has elegant table manners, but does she credit her dad with her sophistication? She won't say.

1.
Prepare Your Child for Big Changes.

Upon my son's graduation from elementary school, we sat and talked about his upcoming years as a high school student. He was leaving a school where he was a big fish in a little pond (three hundred-plus students) and going to a college preparatory high school with twelve hundred students. At this particular school, which required an entrance exam and where not many were accepted, he would be in the company of many highly intelligent peers.

"It will be the best of times and the worst of times," I told Brad, paraphrasing Dickens's classic opening to

A Tale of Two Cities. "You'll be changing both physically and emotionally, and you will become extremely frustrated when adults will tell you you're too young for some things and too old for others. Your hormones will confuse you, and so will adults. You'll feel like you don't fit in."

Brad groaned, and I was afraid I had painted too grim a picture. "But," I hurried on, "some of the greatest times of your life will happen because you'll be spreading your wings and finding your individuality. You'll have newfound freedoms to go places and do things without parental supervision." His eyes lit up, and I hastened to add, "provided you're responsible with that privilege."

"Dad," Brad interrupted, "can we talk about how soon I can get my driver's license?"

2.
SELF-ESTEEM IS TEMPERED BY LIFE'S EXPERIENCES.

Because I wanted to encourage my daughter on her first day in high school, I didn't leave for my law office at the usual time but stayed at the breakfast table to talk with her. "Brenda," I said, looking into her beautiful but still-innocent sapphire eyes, "you're starting a new life today and traveling through that life will be like forging steel. Without the constant heating and cooling, accompanied by tremendous hammering and banging to temper it, it will never reach its true strength. Neither will you. So forge yourself in the forces of life and enjoy it all."

I smiled. Another parental duty well done.

Brenda looked at me with a frown and said, "Huh?"

3.
HELP YOUR CHILD FIND HER
TRUE SELF-IMAGE.

The difference between a negative self-image and an accurate one is the difference between accepting what others think about you versus accepting what God knows about you. We tell our son, "Listen to God."

4.
A GOOD SELF-IMAGE MUST NOT BE
BASED ON OUTWARD BEAUTY.

"Why does the world place so much emphasis on outward beauty?" I asked my teenage daughter. She made me proud when she answered, "Because they're trying to cover up inward ugliness. Mom, you're always telling me to be beautiful on the inside, and then I'll be beautiful outside."

Sometimes they do hear what you say.

5.
SHOW ME THE PERSON YOU ADMIRE, AND I'LL SHOW YOU THE PERSON YOU ARE.

Be a parent your teen will admire. Every child needs someone to look up to. Watch to see whom your child admires because he very likely will become like that person.

6.
POINT OUT HOW SPECIAL THEY ARE.

"God made you special," I often tell my fourteen-year-old son, especially when he's down for some reason. "He had your picture on His wall long before you were born." Then we read Psalm 139 together (verses 14 and 16): "I will praise You, for I am fearfully and wonderfully made. . . . Your eyes saw my substance, being yet unformed. And in Your book they all were written, the days fashioned for me, when as yet there were none of them."

7.
DADS ARE IMPORTANT TO GIRLS.

Daughters need a daily hug, kiss, and "I love you" from Dad. At this time of their life, they are defining their relationship with men. Their cup of love needs to be filled at home by the best male model (hopefully) in their lives—Dad. They are seeking approval from the opposite sex, and if Dad gives them love, they feel secure, and some of the pressure is off. They need to be able to call him at any time they are in trouble, especially if they get into a situation with a boy that is uncomfortable.

8.
DON'T SPANK, PINCH, SLAP, OR PUSH.

When children become teenagers, any kind of physical punishment is degrading to them, even in the privacy of their own home. Their resentment can run deep.

"Why do you treat me like a little kid?" my son roared at me one day. "I'm almost an adult; treat me like an adult and talk to me about how you feel. Don't just push me around. You wouldn't do that to any other adult you were having trouble with."

Good lesson learned. Our relationship improved after I understood his feelings.

9.
DON'T YELL WITHOUT KNOWING WHAT'S GOING ON.

Occasionally my fifteen-year-old son has to take care of his younger brother. More than once, his mother and I have walked in on a scene where the younger boy is hurt or crying, angry or lost. Naturally, our reaction is quick and, usually, loud. Terry has told me, "Why do you and Mom yell at me without knowing what's really going on? Half the time you have it all wrong. But there you are, hollering away before you've even asked me what's happened. It really makes me feel bad about myself."

10.
EACH CHILD NEEDS HIS OWN RELATIONSHIP
WITH A PARENT.

I make it a practice to take each of my four children out once a week to dinner, for ice cream, or to walk through the mall. I feel closer to that child during that time than any other. Oh, sure, we eat dinner together (which a lot of families don't do much anymore), but then everyone is talking, and a child's innermost feelings aren't likely to be shared with the group. I wouldn't give up my personal time getting to know my children for anything.

11.
DON'T STEREOTYPE.

"You're just like your mother. . . . Your brother used to do that very thing. . . . All the kids nowadays are into drugs. . . ."

These are the kinds of things I used to say to my son and daughter until one day my boy lashed out at me: "I'm me, Dad. Me. I'm not Mother; I'm not my brother; I'm not all the other kids. I'm me. Jeff. Me."

12.
EVEN SMALL PRAISE MATTERS.

When fifteen-year-old Chris was given the temporary job of taking the rainfall and temperature readings for the area where we live and phoning them into the nearest weather bureau, he was considerably nervous at this big responsibility. To show him how proud we were of him and how confident we were in his ability to handle the job, I baked his favorite cake for him and put "weatherman" across the top in fudge icing. This bolstered his self-esteem and made him determined to do a good job.

13.
ADMIT YOUR OWN MISTAKES TO YOUR KIDS.

"I love hearing stories of the silly things you and Mom did when you were my age," Mark has said to me many times. "It makes me feel that when I do stupid stuff, I'm not so bad."

14.
SHOW THEM HOW SPECIAL THEY ARE TO YOU.

My kids love to hear stories of what they did when they were little and the funny things they said. So I put together in a book a compilation of this material, and it is their favorite thing to read together. They laugh at the same things over and over.

"Why did you write all this stuff down, Mom?" Laura says to me time and again. It's almost a ritual, her question, because she knows exactly what my answer will be: "Because I love you so much, I don't want to forget a single moment of your life."

15.
REMEMBER TO PRAISE YOUR CHILDREN.

"I'll do something I think is good," a friend of our son says, "and I wait for my mom to praise me, but she doesn't. She expects everything."

The disappointment on his face breaks my heart. He's a good kid and rarely gets into trouble.

"It makes it easier to do things when they're appreciated," he goes on. "Just because they're expected doesn't mean they can't be appreciated."

16.
"Treat Us Like Adults," Our Daughters Tell Us.

"We hate it when we are treated like kids," Susan said to us. Her twin sister Sarah then joined in. "Yeah, but that's a problem. Sometimes I like being treated like a kid. I like to crawl up into Dad's lap."

Susan shrugged her shoulders and looked at her father and me from the corner of her eyes. "I guess you just have to know when we want to be treated like kids and when to treat us like adults," she concluded.

Their father and I smiled and nodded our agreement.

17.
Never Underestimate Kids.

They know more than we parents think they do. It's important to let them know we're aware of their intelligence and common sense. Nothing makes them feel more grown up than that.

18.
How Many Ways Can You Praise Your Child?

I have a paper hanging on the wall of our home-school area. Published by Charter Hospital of Indianapolis, the poster is titled, "101 Ways to Praise a Child." It starts with "Wow. . .Way to go. . .Super. . ." and ends with "You made my day. . . .That's the best. . . . I love you! P.S. Remember, a smile is worth a thousand words!"

I need this constant reminder because I'm not a good praiser.

19.
Praise, Not Criticism, Builds Successful People.

I have a poster on my refrigerator that reads, "Encouragement to children is like rain is to flowers." My children think they can do anything, and so do I. From the time our youngsters were born, we've told them and showed them we love them, that God loves them, that we wanted them in our family, and even prayed for them to come (though during these teen years, we sometimes silently wonder why).

We build into our family life events that feature the talents of each child as an individual, be it music, sports, art, whatever. From choosing paint colors to painting the room to painting murals on the walls, each child has been allowed to decorate his or her own room. The girls each learned to sew at least one dress they could wear (the boys refused!). They all were taught to maintain their cars. They were all given opportunities to excel.

Praise, not criticism, builds successful people. We encourage, praise, and reward for good behavior. Our children have used their healthy self-esteem to get them through personal tragedies, social problems, and work difficulties.

A word of caution, though: False praise and flattery will do more harm than good. Teach children first, help them succeed by guiding, cajoling, and rewarding, and when they have chosen correctly, lather them with affection, always pointing out what they did right.

20.
CREATE A FAMILY AND CREATE SELF-ESTEEM.

Every Monday night, we have a family meeting. We stay together as a family and do family-centered things. We don't answer the phone, entertain friends, or plan to be gone on Mondays. The evenings were short when the children were younger, considering their attention span, and may have consisted of a special story, short video, or trip to the park.

Now that the kids are older—four teenagers and a ten year old—we do more challenging things: how to change a tire, how to sew, how to budget money, how to iron a shirt. Every week is different. We divide the month into four subjects. The first week is a religious lesson. The second week is an activity outside the home, the third week a how-to lesson or activity, and the fourth a physical activity such as basketball, softball, or bowling.

Sometimes we watch Monday Night Football or order in pizza and have serious discussions on social problems. These discussions often last two or three hours.

These family nights have built us into a strong, cohesive group of individuals who know they can depend on each other. We know each other's strengths and vulnerabilities. Most of all, though, we know we love and care for each other, and that God is the head of our home, the silent witness to every action, the silent listener to every conversation.

21.
PARENTS OF TEENS NEED SELF-ESTEEM, TOO

As part of my research for a book I'm writing on disease and how it affects family life, I began discussing with my teenage daughter the way publishing works. Janice asked if I were going to make any money from the book.

"I hope so," I answered, "but my main purpose in writing it is to create awareness and help others."

Janice looked at me as though I were crazy. "Well, Mom, I think you should make some money, at least enough to hire a housekeeper since you never clean anymore."

22.
Don't Criticize Your Kids in Front of Their Siblings or Friends.

Teenagers are sensitive beings who feel words far more than we realize, especially when those words make them look stupid, incompetent, or bad. It's better to take the child aside and talk to him privately than berate him in front of others. You'll destroy self-esteem fast if you criticize him in front of others.

23.
Nourish Your Child's Self-Esteem Rather Than Tear It Down.

My husband has a short temper. When he gets mad, he says things he regrets later and then nicely apologizes. Unfortunately, the words can't be erased from the mind, and our thirteen-year-old son Ryan is sensitive and often thinks his dad's anger is his fault. Sometimes it is, but most of the time it isn't. Ryan is afraid of his father's temper, and his self-esteem is suffering.

24.
TEENS LOVE GOING TO FANCY RESTAURANTS.

Whenever our daughter works especially hard around the house, we reward her by taking her to an elegant restaurant. She likes getting dressed up and playing the part of the sophisticated young woman. "We noticed all that you've done for the family this week, and want to show our appreciation," we explain to her.

25.
DOING WELL IN SCHOOL BOOSTS SELF-ESTEEM.

When my oldest was in kindergarten, I asked his teacher how she had raised her three children to be straight-A students through high school. She told me that every summer, until junior high, she gave each child a simple daily worksheet reviewing skills they had learned that year. It took them less than a half-hour to complete and did not introduce any new concepts.

When school started in the fall, her children were prepared and ready to learn; they had not lost any ground. They also were not "burned out" from too much work.

I used this method with both my sons through junior high, and now that they're in high school I have them read library books in the summer. Michael, my oldest, is graduating this year as valedictorian. Matthew, a freshman, seems to be following in his brother's footsteps.

That teacher's method really works!

26.
WRITE AN ESSAY ON YOUR CHILD; LET HIM READ IT.

When my son applied to be a foreign exchange student in his senior year of high school, both of us had to write an essay on such topics as his character, discipline, his future, and my parenting style. What an experience to sit down and write about my son! So often as parents, we complain about little things, but how refreshing it is to write about the good things.

When Jeremy read what I'd written, he was surprised at how I really felt about him, and he thanked me for being such a good and patient mom.

Then I got to read his essay and was thrilled at what he said about my parenting: "The best part about being in this family is that my mom makes a hot meal every night, and we all sit around the table together and eat without the TV being on, and we talk."

Write a letter to your child. It may be easier to express your positive feelings on paper than face to face. I'm sure it will give a boost to your relationship.

SEX

The thoughts of the wicked are an abomination to the LORD, but the words of the pure are pleasant.

PROVERBS 15:26

Ten-year-old David heard strange sounds coming from outside his bedroom window. The sounds got louder and turned out to be voices—those of his sixteen-year-old brother Terry and Terry's girlfriend, Linda.

David stopped doing his homework at his desk and went to the window to look out. What he saw was more than he'd bargained for.

Later that day, David found Terry in the kitchen. "Thanks, Terry," he said to him.

"For what?"

"For—how should I put it—the education?"

"What are you talking about?" Terry was getting perturbed at David's little game.

"I saw you and Linda."

Terry's eyes narrowed. "Saw us where?"

"On the swing in the backyard."

Terry's mouth dropped open. "Where were you? I didn't hear you come out."

"I was in my room doing my homework." David smiled. "I'll bet Mom and Dad would be interested in hearing what I saw today, me, a ten-year-old kid, and in my own backyard!"

"Why you little. . ." Terry threatened, moving toward David.

David held up his hand to stop his brother. "I won't tell on you, Terry."

"Oh, yeah? What's it going to cost me?"

David grinned. "How about taking out the garbage all this week? That oughtta erase my memory."

"Terry," I said a day or so later when I was in the kitchen mopping the floor, "how come you're taking out the garbage? I thought that was David's job."

He gave me his sweetest smile. "Just wanted to help, Mom."

(Note: See last page of this chapter for recommended Christian literature on teenagers and sex.)

1.
PREMARITAL SEX DESTROYS
THE FOUNDATION OF TRUST.

We warned Amy that premarital sex would hurt more than help a relationship with a person she cared about, or thought she loved. "He may act as though he's glad you've given in to him, but he'll always wonder if you've done it before, even if you say you haven't."

I continued, "If he thinks you don't have enough self-control to say no to him now, he will take advantage of you in all areas, all the time. And soon he will tire of someone with no mind of her own, someone not able to think for herself. Such a situation may be the precursor of an abusive relationship or marriage."

2.
BOYS USE THE SAME LINES TODAY
THAT THEY DID IN YOUR DAY.

Men and women don't change much when it comes to sex and what one has to do to get it. Guys will talk "love" to get sex, and girls will give sex to get love. "Both strategies are wrong," we told our daughter, "because they're aimed at using the other person to get what is wanted. You could very well sacrifice your virginity for a security he won't give you after all."

3.
THE DIFFERENCE BETWEEN LOVE, ROMANCE, AND LUST.

I had a heart-to-heart talk with my son about his body and the sexual tension he was starting to feel. "Romance is the warm, fuzzy feeling that fades when the novelty wears off," I told him. "Lust is nothing more than giving in to an animalistic craving, with no thought of feelings or caring. Love, on the other hand, is a verb. It puts into action a commitment to a relationship and does what is best for the other person. The next time you think you're 'falling in love' with a girl, ask yourself if it's love or lust or romance."

4.
LET YOUR CHILD KNOW SEX IS A BEAUTIFUL THING.

I had a discussion with my daughter about sex when she was fourteen. "When I was growing up," I told her, "sex was thought of as dirty, and I received all negative information about it. But since becoming an adult, and especially after becoming a Christian and being married, I learned that sex is a beautiful gift from God when shared by two people who love each other and are committed to each other in marriage."

We discussed together the reasons why girls give up their virginity instead of saving it for their life's partner. We talked about AIDS and pregnancy, and she responded openly. I was treating her with respect by asking for her opinions, too.

I told her I hoped she would wait for marriage before having sex, but if she didn't, though I would be disappointed, I would not stop loving her or wanting to be with her.

Teresa is getting married in two weeks and yes, she saved herself for marriage. "You explained to me how precious sex can be between two people who want to experience it for all the right reasons," she told me recently. "I wanted that special relationship built on commitment."

5.
TEENS CAN DO WITHOUT SEX UNTIL MARRIAGE.

My son, Jeremy, has taken an oath before God, me, and the church that he will not have sex before marriage. He told me once that the promise has taken so much pressure off of him while dating.

6.
BEWARE OF FLIRTING.

Flirting is a sin because it defrauds, meaning such an action sensually exposes a boy or girl to what they can't have morally.

Sex is within marriage only. God hasn't changed His position on this, even though the world has. As much as it has become accepted to sleep with whomever one wants, such a morally corrupt action will never be less than sin in God's eyes. Sex drives can be encouraged or downplayed and controlled. This is part of the self-control of the Christian. It may not be a popular view, but it is the Bible's view.

7.
TALK ABOUT SEX.

Sex is a natural part of life. If you don't talk much about sex when kids are younger, you will be extremely uncomfortable with the subject when they're teen-agers (and they will, too), when you really do need to talk about it.

You know your kids will get information on sex from somewhere. Wouldn't you rather it came from you?

8.
TEENS NEED SUPPORT
TO KEEP FROM HAVING SEX.

My son belongs to a Baptist church that promotes a program called "True Love Waits." A youth counselor has meetings with the teens to explain why it is best to wait until marriage to have sex and that it will be a mighty blessing from the Lord if they do.

The kids make this promise to God and to their parents in front of the entire congregation. Even if they have had sex before, they can ask the Lord for forgiveness and make the promise.

The teens I have seen who make this promise are stronger in their beliefs and very close to one another. They can talk to each other about their problems, and their youth counselor is always available to them. They also know they can talk to their parents if they are being tempted.

9.
IF YOU FIND OUT THE WORST
HAS HAPPENED. . .

It wasn't hard for Jim and me to see that Anne was in love for the first time. Although we didn't think she and

Dale were a good match for each other, we did our best to be tolerant and hoped the relationship would soon be over. She had become a Christian the year before, and her Christian life meant a great deal to her. She was active in the youth group and on the Bible Bowl team. She loved and respected us—we had tried hard to be good examples—and she knew right from wrong.

We started taking Dale, her boyfriend, to church with us every Sunday. He learned of God's plan of salvation from Anne and the youth group and had recently decided to be baptized. Several nights a week I was letting him visit at our house until 10 p.m. because they wanted more time together.

Her father and I had talked with Anne in depth about how guys and girls react to each other and why she shouldn't put herself in a tempting situation. We thought we had all the bases covered.

Jim and I were devastated, then, to discover she was sneaking out at night to meet Dale and that they had had sex five times. "It's a compulsion for me," Anne told us.

Our whole family—we have two other children—suffered a traumatic change. The trust we used to have, as parents for our children, turned into fear and suspicion. Love was still our motive, though, and we prayed continuously for God to guide us.

There was the trip to the doctor's to find out if Anne had been exposed to an S.T.D. (sexually transmitted disease). She was given a home pregnancy test which was negative.

Dale, Anne, Jim, and I, and Dale's stepfather met around our dining room table to discuss the situation. For me, this was one of the hardest things I've ever done. We talked about what had been going on. Jim made it clear that we and Dale's stepfather would be working together to make sure Anne and Dale weren't together unsupervised again. As much as we wanted to, we didn't forbid them from seeing each other because we were afraid they would run away. At the time Dale was sixteen and Anne, fifteen.

Jim told them we would not give our consent for them to be married until Anne was eighteen. If they still wanted to marry then, we would give our approval. Jim knew that a lot can change in three years, and it did.

In just a little over a year Anne and Dale grew away from each other. I thank God for my husband's wisdom and self-control.

10.
ACCEPT THE FACT THAT THIS GENERATION IS DIFFERENT FROM YOURS.

I hate having to talk to my son about sex, AIDS, homosexuality, drug and alcohol abuse, and random violence. I wish he were growing up in a world where all this ugliness wasn't on the front page of the newspaper or the television news every day. The reality is, it's a different world. Oh, sure, those problems have always existed, but not to the blatant degree we witness today.

As Brandon's father, I don't dare ignore the fact that

he has to grow up a lot sooner than I did. If I don't give him my Christian perspective on these situations, whom can I trust to do so? It's my responsibility because Brandon is my son—not the school's, not the church's, not the community's. I know parents today have less and less authority over their own children, but I'm going to be an influence in Brandon's life as much as I can, with God's help.

11.
CHRISTIAN LITERATURE CAN HELP TEACH ABOUT SEX.

We've used a terrific series of books by Concordia Publishing House titled Learning About Sex. There are six books in the series, and it starts with information appropriate to share with three to five year olds, then six to eight, eight to eleven, eleven to fourteen, and fourteen and older. For ages eleven to fourteen, the appropriate book is *Sex and the New You,* and for those fourteen and older, the book is *Love, Sex, and God.*

12.
TALK ABOUT DELICATE SUBJECTS WITH YOUR KIDS BEFORE SOMEONE ELSE DOES.

At an early age, children learn about sex and other subjects (homosexuality, rape) from a variety of sources. We didn't want to be the last ones to give our opinions on these important subjects, so we started at an early age watching for opportunities and our children's natural curiosity to discuss these matters with them.

13.
DON'T OVERLOAD KIDS WITH INFORMATION.

When five-year-old Brandon asked why my stomach was growing, that was the perfect time to explain about a new baby arriving. He asked simple questions; I answered in kind. I didn't give him a six-week course on reproduction.

Now that Brandon is a teenager, there are many subjects we've already discussed that have to do with his changing body. Again, we encourage his questions, and we answer those questions directly. It's not easy being specific with certain information, but we gauge how much to tell Brandon by his curiosity and what we feel he's likely to face at his age. Again, we don't overload him beyond what he's interested in or needs to know at that moment in time.

14.
BE A PARENT YOUR CHILD
CAN APPROACH ABOUT SEX.

Thirteen-year-old Christine told me about a friend of hers who said she was going to have sex with her boyfriend at her home soon. Both parents worked, so it would be easy to do. Christine wanted me to do something about it to keep it from happening.

Now, maybe some parents wouldn't want to get involved, but I didn't hesitate because I would want to know if my thirteen year old were experimenting with sex.

I made some inquiries and found out Christine's friend was known to lie and boast about doing things she never did. Still, Christine believed she was really going to do it.

At the same time, I was told by neighbors that the child was properly supervised at all times and was never alone in the house. I chose to believe she was just trying to act grown up, and I didn't get involved.

Turns out, she was just making up the story, and she got mad at Christine for telling me. Later I talked with her gently and explained that Christine was being a true friend in wanting to keep her from getting into trouble. Thankfully, she understood that, and she and Christine are still friends, and both are wiser from the experience.

15.
Introduce Courting.

Joshua Harris's book, *I Kissed Dating Good-bye,* had a profound influence on my daughter. She read it, then sent him an E-mail thanking him for writing what she also believed about dating.

The gist of the book is to wait to begin "courting" until you're ready to look for a life partner, financially secure enough to get married, and old enough to be emotionally prepared. Before that, dating is out. According to Harris, dating simply sets up youngsters for experiences they're just not ready for.

Going out with groups is good, and getting to know boys while others are around is best. Having a good time with a bunch of kids during the teen years is better than serious dating.

My daughter agrees with this concept and is going to wait until she's ready for marriage before she allows herself to get serious with a young man.

16.
A Gold Wedding Band Will Remind Your Teen to Wait Until Marriage to Have Sex.

On the day that our daughter Chelsi stood at the front of the church—before God, the members, the minister, and her mother and me—and vowed to wait until marriage before having sex, we gave her a plain gold wedding band. She wears it on her right hand as a constant reminder that her decision was not a light one, taken on the spur of the moment, but that she wants to be held responsible for her vow.

On her wedding day, if she chooses, she can give the ring to her new husband, as her gift to him of her purity.

17.
BOYS CAN WEAR A GOLD MEDALLION TO SHOW THEIR COMMITMENT TO PURITY UNTIL MARRIAGE.

When our son made a vow to remain chaste until his wedding day, instead of giving him a ring, which some parents do, we got him a gold medallion to wear on a chain around his neck. He doesn't hide it under a shirt but wears it on the outside for all the world to see.

18.
What to Say to Your Child if She Breaks Her Vow to Remain Pure until Married.

There are many teenagers in our church who have vowed not to have sex until marriage. We were pleased when our daughter wanted to make this vow.

"We support you in this 100 percent," we told her. "But if you break that vow, we want you to know that though we'll be disappointed, we'll still love you, and so will God. He won't turn His back on you, and neither will we."

She knows we don't say this to make it easier for her to break her commitment, but so that she knows she can come to us with any confession, and we won't disown her.

19.
Teens are Smarter Than Parents Think.

When I asked my daughter why she hadn't brought a boy around the house lately, her answer surprised me. "Why should I get into a relationship with a guy at this point in my life? I'm not ready for marriage; I certainly don't want children, and it's just too easy to get into trouble."

Her simple explanation helped me know not to urge

her to go out, thinking she needs male companionship. I'm pleased to find that Tracy knows what's best for Tracy at this age.

20.
Don't Worry, You'll Know When It's Time to Have the Talk.

I wondered about whether I'd know the right time to talk to my son about sex. I didn't want to do it too late or too early. Frankly, I didn't want to do it at all. But my wife pointed the finger at me, and so I waited for a cue of some kind that would tell me "It's time." It came unexpectedly one night at the dinner table when five-year-old Bradley said, "If girls get periods, what do boys get? Commas?" He was totally serious. I knew it was time.

21.
Answer Only Age-Appropriate Sex Questions.

As my daughter has been growing up, she's been exposed, despite our careful screening, to sexual words, innuendoes, and graphic situations on television in the movies. When she asks an age-appropriate question— "What does that mean, Mom?"—I'll answer it. If I feel she's not ready for that knowledge, I'll simply say, "That has to do with sex, and is not something you need to understand," or "When you get older, we can discuss it."

Now that she's a teenager, we are discussing those delicate situations.

22.
How to Get Rid of "The Mood."

I asked Casey how she and Bryan, her boyfriend, handle sexual temptation. She said, "When I feel the mood coming on, I'll say, 'Okay. . .,' and Bryan will finish the sentence by saying, 'Let's go do something else.'" Sometimes they read the Bible together. Casey says, "That really gets rid of 'the mood.'"

23.
Think Ahead.

My daughter, Ann, told me, "My version of making out is kissing, hugging, and hands on the back and shoulders. Once you feel the urge to grope, you know it's time to stop. It's so hard, but then you think *Mom*, and the temptation disappears. We'll be sitting there kissing, and Ben will look behind me and say, 'Hi, Mom,' and it kills the mood. He's done it so many times he says he's going to be like the boy who cried wolf, only he's the boy who cries 'Mom'! One day I won't believe him, and I'll say, 'Yeah, right,' and keep on kissing him. He'll say, 'Ann, your mom really is standing at the door.'"

We laughed, and I suggested that her dad and I get a large portrait made of us and hang it in the room. Ann said, "The desire will always be there; we just think ahead."

24.
DON'T BELIEVE THE ONE-LINERS!

One year ago my daughter, Christina, and I weren't getting along very well. She was fifteen and in a destructive relationship with a non-Christian. Her father and I wanted her out of it badly, but we knew we couldn't make it happen. She would have to decide it was time. I was miserable and searched for ways to pull her away from this boy, Paul.

In an attempt to mend our relationship, Christina and I went to a counselor. This therapist, who was too young to have children of her own, basically told me to get a life. By the end of the second visit, I was so mad that Christina and I decided not to go back. That was the only thing we agreed on for six months.

My husband handled it much better than I did but certainly wasn't any happier. He was afraid if we forbade Christina and Paul to see each other, they'd run away.

He continued to bring Paul with us to church and allowed them to have supervised visits with each other. I was an emotional wreck, and Christina was, too.

Now, a year and a half later, we can talk about it. She told me, "Unfortunately, maturity and wisdom come from bad experiences and mistakes." My beautiful little girl grew up. I had hoped and tried to protect her from mistakes and the pain they cause, but I couldn't.

I asked her what advice she would give other young women about how to deal with sex. She said emphatically, "It's not as good as he'll make it out to be! When you don't want to go to bed with him, but you're doing it because he wants to, that's stupid. And, don't believe the one-liners: 'It's okay; everybody does it; if you love me you will; you don't want to be a virgin all your life, do you?'

"If he puts pressure on you to have sex with him, and you don't want to, you shouldn't be in this relationship. You shouldn't even be with him. If he tries to force you to have sex, scream as loud as you can. Kick, bite, punch, claw his eyes out, do anything you can to get away. If he loves you, he won't act like that. If he tries to force you, he doesn't care about you; all he cares about is himself."

25.
"Why Give Away Your Most Precious Gift."

I told my daughters that their lives would change forever the moment they gave away their most precious gift: their virginity. "Since this is such a special occasion," I told them, "it should be reserved for a very special young man. That is why God intended the 'first time' to occur on a woman's wedding night. Sex before marriage is a sin. Period."

I feel it's a parental obligation to spell out the correct use of sex to children.

Recommended Christian literature on the subject of teenagers and sex:

Facing the Facts by Stanton L. Jones, Stan Jones, and Brenna B. Jones. Colorado Springs: NavPress, 1995.

I Kissed Dating Good-bye by Joshua Harris. Sisters, OR: Multnomah, 1997.

Learning about Sex (six-book series). St. Louis: Concordia Publishing House, 1988.

Old Enough To Know by Michael W. Smith and Fritz Ridenour. Worthy Publishers, 1987.

Setting You Free to Make Right Choices: Workbook for Junior High and High School Students by Josh McDowell. Nashville: Broadman and Holman Publishers, 1995.

Why Wait?: What You Need to Know about the Teen Sexuality Crisis by Josh McDowell and Dick Day. Nashville: Thomas Nelson Publishers, 1994.

SIBLING RIVALRY

Better is a dry morsel with quietness, than a house full of feasting with strife.

PROVERBS 17:1

The squabbling between brother and sister started in the morning; that was nothing new. Ken and I, as a rule, stayed out of such tiffs and let the kids work it through themselves—if possible.

At noon I heard them again, voices raised, tones strident. It had something to do with a telephone call not reported. Lisa was the aggressor. David had done something she wasn't soon going to let him forget.

By three o'clock, I had two angry teenagers. The

exchange between them when they passed each other in the hallway by the kitchen was hot. Faces were red.

"Is there something we need to talk about together?" Ken asked them the question that was on the tip of my tongue. I could tell the problem was not going away by itself.

"No, Dad," David said, throwing his shoulders back and charging out the back door.

"Lisa?" I questioned my redheaded daughter.

"He's a jerk. What more can I say?" She stormed out the front door.

"I have to make a quick trip to the repair shop to pick up my lawn mower," Ken told me. "When I get back, we'd better sit down with Lisa and David and get this conflict settled."

"Okay," I agreed. I went to the garage to do some laundry.

Ken came home in twenty minutes, met me in the garage, and together we walked into the kitchen to see if either of the kids was there. Nope. As I started down the hallway toward their rooms, which were side by side, my eyes caught a gaping, splintered hole in the hall closet door. Something had plowed through it. Fiercely. Ken saw it, too.

David charged in from the backyard, still seething over something. "Whoa, Sport," Ken said as he stopped him. "What's happened here?"

We both gestured toward the shattered door and, in that moment, I knew what had happened. "I suppose there's a logical explanation for how your fist got through this door?" I questioned.

"Better the door than Lisa's face."

His answer shocked me, but I understood. David

was a kid you could push a long ways before his temper would get the better of him. Lisa must have really pushed. In a way, I appreciated his resolve not to do bodily harm when he'd reached his limit.

"I want this door fixed. Now!" Ken told him.

David looked truly remorseful. "Yes, Sir. Sorry, Dad. Mom."

Ken and David stared stared at each other a minute, father and son. I figured Ken was thinking, *Should I ground him, yell at him, or force him to apologize to Lisa?* Recognizing that there had been a few times in my own life when rage had made me want to destroy. . .something, but I'd chosen a safer way to let out the frustration, I decided David's action was not the beginning of dangerous behavior.

Apparently, Ken thought so, too. "You could have broken your hand," he said quietly.

David nodded, his head lowered. "I'll get the tools I need to repair this door."

Ken and I both nodded okay.

Today, as grownups, David and Lisa are the best of friends. They're tight, as their generation says. But there were times. . . .

1.
DO UNTO OTHERS STILL WORKS.

Our daughters are eight years apart, and for that reason we have encouraged Jennifer to become a model for her younger sister. We remind her that Allison looks up to her and admires her more than she realizes. We hope she will set a good example, one of love and maturity. But at times, when she mistreats Allison or is impatient with her, we ask her how she would feel if we were to treat her like that. The old Golden Rule applies here: "Do unto others as you would have others do unto you."

2.
DON'T COMPARE SIBLINGS.

My daughter has told me that one of the worst things I do as a parent is to compare her to her sister, who is two years older. "You're always urging me to be as smart, as well mannered, and as clothes-conscious as Stacy. That puts me under pressure to be Stacy but not me. I want to be me, Mom."

3.
KIDS KNOW WHEN YOU HAVE FAVORITES.

What more do I need to say?

4.
THE TEEN YEARS STARTED THE SIBLING RIVALRY.

Our two boys were the best of playmates growing up, but now that the older boy is a teenager, things have changed. They are two very different boys with different goals. This change mystified us until we realized that Tom is dealing with teenage situations, and, to him, Teddy is still a child. A baby. The older boy is often intolerant of his little brother's attempts to be his friend and buddy.

Tom wants his own space, his own possessions. Teddy doesn't understand that or respect it. Tom is his big brother; they've always shared everything.

We mediate when necessary, knowing we can't dictate Tom's attitude toward his younger brother. We forbid certain behavior such as yelling at each other, name calling, and hitting.

Tom simply moved into a sphere where Teddy doesn't fit and can't follow—yet. We try to understand Tom's growing pains.

5.
BECOME YOUR CHILD'S ATTORNEY.

When Brooke and Darcy hit their teen years—they're just eleven months apart—it seemed like overnight they lost the ability to be together for two minutes without arguing. They grumble about each other's doings, and their father and I are caught in the middle.

Since Mike is an attorney, he came up with this idea: When a situation erupts into something serious enough to need mediation, he puts the two girls in a room alone for fifteen minutes to talk through their differences. There is no yelling allowed, and each one has a fair share of time to explain her feelings, as they must stay together for fifteen minutes.

If this doesn't solve the problem, then either he or I talk privately with one girl, then the other, and then we put them together again, and the adult mediates. The purpose is to solve differences without violence or name calling. Such an approach works about 80 percent of the time.

Don't ask how we solve the other 20 percent. We haven't figured that out yet.

6.
RIVALRY IS INEVITABLE
WHEN YOU HAVE TWO TEENAGERS.

Our sons are two and a half years apart, and talk about sibling rivalry! When they get angry, the first thing they do is call each other names, something we stop quickly, if we hear it. They're not allowed to put each other down, either, especially if they're out with friends. "Never forget that you're brothers; you should stick up for each other," we urge them.

7.
PHYSICAL ACTIVITY
OFTEN COOLS TEMPERS.

Both our sons take karate. When they start going at each other, I tell them, "Go put on your sparring equipment and go outside." It's funny, but when we give them permission to be physically aggressive with each other, it cools them down, and they're no longer interested in fighting it out.

8.

WHEN YOU HAVE A PERFECT CHILD. . .

Thirteen-year-old Greg is organized, bright, makes good grades, and is adept at just about anything he tries, whether it be music, sports, or even household chores. His older brother, Eric, on the other hand, does most things differently. Trouble comes when Greg tries to impart his "perfectness" on his brother. "You're not doing it right. . . . Let me show you how to do it" is a familiar refrain. Eric is pretty easygoing but doesn't like "the kid," as he calls his younger brother, telling him what to do.

I step in before it gets out of hand and tell them to cool down and get their minds focused on something else. Sometimes I can diffuse the situation by showing them they are both right in the way they're doing something. They're just seeing the solution from different perspectives.

Not surprisingly, my husband handles these situations in his own way. He won't interfere except to say, "Just get the kitchen cleaned up. I don't want to hear any fussing." He believes they have to learn to work together, but at the same time they know he's within earshot of their conversations.

I'm not sure which method works the best, but both are effective.

9.
BUILD ON EACH CHILD'S STRENGTHS.

We're careful to find each child's abilities and then praise and encourage them. Such an attitude lessens the rivalry between them and helps build self-esteem.

10.
HANG ON.
THEY MAY LIKE EACH OTHER MORE THAN YOU KNOW.

A man hates to hear his children squabbling. My kids do it all the time, usually nitpicking rather than engaging in outright battles. It drives me nuts! But then, every once in awhile, I'll overhear them having a reasonable conversation, and I'll think, *There's hope for them yet.*

11.
REMIND THE KIDS OF THE BOND THEY SHARE.

"We are a family," I often remind my three children, two of whom are teenagers. "There is an incredible bond that connects us, and we need to know we can depend on each other to be there, no matter what, to support and understand." I emphasize that bond all I can.

12.
"You're Not Fair."

How many times have you heard one of your children accuse you of playing favorites? "You're always picking on me. . . . You let him do that, why can't I?. . . Why does he get a bigger allowance than I do?"

"You're different people," I tell my son and daughter. "I'm going to do some things with Amanda that I won't do with Paddy. It may seem like I'm doing more for one of you than the other, but I try not to. It evens out in the long run."

If I take Amanda on a shopping date, I'll bring something back for her younger brother, to let him know that I'm thinking of him. If I'm with Paddy, I'll bring Amanda a sack of her favorite candy.

13.
Give It Time.

Jeanie is usually good at seeing the other person's viewpoint, except when that person is her sister Maria. Jeanie says she likes to treat people the way she wants to be treated—and she can't stand it when Maria, who is three and a half years younger, doesn't follow suit.

I'm proud of Jeanie's attitude because a few years ago she thought of herself first. I talked to her many times about putting others first and treating them the way she would want to be treated. She had to learn to think how the other person would feel because of what she said or did.

Now Maria is struggling through the same learning process. This must be why parents get gray hair. Although she would never admit it, I can see that Maria admires Jeanie and tries to be like her, although they are complete opposites.

With God's guidance, I am sure we will come through this, scarred but victorious.

14.
THERE'S NO ROOM FOR A SUPERSTAR IN OUR HOUSE.

With two teenagers sitting at our dinner table, the family setting for talking about one's day, my husband and I have to consciously defer attention from our oldest child who has been blessed a thousand times over with talent. Her younger sister, Jennifer, is painfully aware of her lack of accomplishments and has accepted a supporting role, often sitting silently while the conversation encompasses "the star."

We do our best, though, to focus attention on Jennifer,

and praise her for her efforts and to offer positive encouragement. We make sure she is included in the discussions and, little by little, she is beginning to initiate topics that explore what has happened to her that day.

15.
DEFUSE SITUATIONS
OF RIVALRY.

My kids were best friends and did everything together until they got into high school. Crystal was a freshman when Katy was a senior. It was a tough time for Katy because her little sister was cute and funny and attracted a lot of attention from Katy's pals. Suddenly, there was resentment on both sides—from Katy who found her baby sister more popular than she, and from Crystal who didn't understand why she couldn't play with the big kids.

I pretty much stayed out of it until Katy's senior prom when a boy in her class asked Crystal to go with him. That's one time I stepped in and said, "*No*, you're not going to Katy's prom. Not with Billy. Not at *all.*" She wasn't happy, but I figured one day she would have her own prom.

After that the rivalry died a quick and painless death. No more competition.

16.
OUR SONS DON'T AGREE ON WHAT GIRLS TO DATE.

When I was growing up, my parents, who were not Christians, thought they knew who would be good for me to date. They didn't understand that I only wanted to date Christian girls. Consequently, I didn't do much dating in high school. When I went away to college, and my parents weren't around to push their opinions on me, I only dated Christian girls and eventually married my wife, who is a Christian.

One of my sons feels the same way about dating, while the other one wants to have nothing to do with Christian girls. This has caused some rivalry and bitter feelings between the brothers because we seem to be favoring one over the other even though we're striving to be fair to both.

17.
EXERCISE BURNS OFF FRUSTRATION.

Have you ever noticed that when you're angry you want to do something physical—like punch, swing, stomp, run, or kick? When our youngsters get physically aggressive with each other, we take that energy and channel it constructively, using several exercise machines in the garage. When they need discipline, our sons hear this: "To the garage. Lift some weights. Punch the bag."

18.
HEALTHY DOSES OF VITAMIN "N"
NEVER HURT.

Vitamin N is the "No" vitamin. It must be liberally given while teenagers roam your house. If you have more than one child, what you allow the oldest one to get away with will double, triple, and even quadruple with each younger sibling. The younger ones watch the older ones, and the cry is heard everywhere: "You let Christy do it!"

Your reply of "You're not Christy!" doesn't hold water. Just be consistent, and do not hesitate in administering liberal doses of Vitamin N. It is okay to say no. If you can, put up a poster on a kitchen wall that says, "What part of 'No' don't you understand?"

19.
MONEY TALKS.

Our oldest son, James, is the messy one; his brother, Rolf is the neat one. They share a room which, for several years, was spic-and-span on one side and cluttered on the other. We tried and tried to get James to be tidier, but we couldn't get a handle on how to get him to pick up after himself.

One time, out of complete frustration, neat Rolf opened the window and tossed out all of sloppy James's "stuff" that was on the floor. Naturally, hostility ensued. We had to come up with a solution.

We decided to have James pay Rolf to keep the room clean and neat. James wasn't thrilled with the idea, but we gave him no choice. Money was garnered from his salary earned at the fast-food restaurant—unless he wanted to do his own cleaning. He didn't and was actually glad not to have the responsibility, and peace reigned between the brothers.

This system has worked well for two years.

20.
FAMILY TIME IS IMPORTANT.

Teenagers are still kids, kids who need fun times interacting with their siblings to nurture relationships. Brothers and sisters could very well be best friends in adulthood. They need to laugh often with the family and eat supper together. We have made Thursday or Friday a "steak" night. We don't always have steak, but we do have something extra special that the kids love to eat. They truly look forward to our doing something together that night. This interaction cuts down on sibling squabbling.

AFTERWORD
Take a Deep Breath...and Pray

> *Trust in the LORD with all your heart,*
> *and lean not on your own understanding;*
> *in all your ways acknowledge Him,*
> *and He shall direct your paths.*
>
> PROVERBS 3:5–6

Most conflicts between parent and child mentioned in this book will be resolved with love, patience, perseverance, and wisdom from God's leading. But what if they aren't? What if you suspect your child may be suffering from depression or anxiety or horribly low self-esteem? What if he or she has threatened suicide or attempted it? What if your son or daughter is addicted to alcohol or drugs or sex?

What can you do when you no longer have the answers?

Early diagnosis is vital in successfully treating psychological and emotional problems and mental health disorders. Sadly, people both young and old don't receive the treatment they need because they or their guardians are ashamed to ask for help; they don't know how to diagnose their symptoms, and/or they aren't aware of nearby available resources.

Should you find yourself as a parent in this situation—you know your child needs professional help—here are a few suggestions that may steer you in the right direction:

(1) Contact your local pastor, or the pastor of a Bible-believing church with an active youth program. If he is a trained counselor, his guidance may be all you need to treat your problem. Or, he may be able to recommend Christian therapists in your area. Perhaps there's even one in your congregation.

(2) Call Focus on the Family at 1-800-232-6459 (1-800-A FAMILY). This organization, presided over by the Christian psychologist and author Dr. James C. Dobson, offers counseling by phone and help in finding the resources you need. To connect directly with counseling resources, call 1-719-531-3400 extension 2700 and a counselor will return your call. All counseling services by phone are free.

(3) Call New Life Ministries (formerly Minirth-Meier Clinic) at 1-800-639-5433 (1-800-NEW LIFE). Christian counselors will determine the level of care you need and will refer you to a clinic or counselor in your local area. No counseling is given over the phone.

(4) Call the Crystal Cathedral at 1-714-639-4673 (1-714-NEW HOPE). Lines are open 24 hours a day, 7 days a week. This organization, founded by well-known

pastor, author, and speaker Dr. Robert Schuller, professes that "a professionally trained and loving person is here waiting to take your call and listen to you." Online (www.newhopeonline.org) you can chat privately with a New Hope counselor seven days a week, twenty-four hours a day. Teenagers who need support can chat teen-to-teen through Teenline.

Remember the words of the Apostle Paul: "For God has not given us a spirit of fear, but of power and of love and of a sound mind" (2 Timothy 1:7).

1.
Where Has My Sweet Child Gone?

I think every parent is surprised to find their thirteen year old is nothing like the twelve year old who went to bed the night before. We know we taught them all the things they are now questioning, but we wonder where they were for those first lessons and why we are having to tell them all over again.

2.
Let God Be the CEO in Your Corporate Family.

There is nowhere you can go to learn to be a parent; it is something you were called by God to do. That's why it is imperative that God be allowed to be your chief executive officer in this management position. There is no shame in that! And remember, you are only human—a sinner, like everyone else. You will make mistakes. But healing comes and growing occurs when there is forgiveness.

3.
LISTEN. . .
WHEN TEENS WANT TO TALK.

With our first teenager, Jay, I was an overeager mother. If he went out, I would be waiting to hear a blow-by-blow account of the event, immediately. This made him clam up, especially if I made a value judgment on his behavior. I learned to wait patiently and feign nonchalance. Usually he couldn't contain himself, and he ended up telling me things anyway.

Our second son, Scott, doesn't discuss his feelings easily. I hang around the kitchen while he is doing the dishes—and then he starts to talk. In this setting we have even talked in detail about sex.

Our youngest, Nick, doesn't express himself unless he feels comfortable with the situation. When he was with his father and me alone on a long car trip recently, he used the cover of darkness and the intimate atmosphere to ask "very important questions" about his relationship with his girlfriend. We had a wonderful, unhurried talk as the miles went by.

One key to communication with your teenager is to establish a nonthreatening, comfortable atmosphere. We learned to be available for our kids, even in the little moments.

4.
MAKE SERVING THE LORD NUMBER ONE.

Kids see hypocrisy. You have to live the Christian life for them to buy it. Never forget you have the best child training manual known to humanity—the Bible. *Use It, over and over.*

5.
PROMISE YOUR KIDS
ABSOLUTE HONESTY.

One of the most important aspects of raising teens is honesty. I make sure I do not lie to them about anything or to anyone else, either. Jim and Jared know they can get an honest answer from me. At times, it's not an easy vow to keep, but it's worth it when I know my children can trust my word.

6.
SHARE YOUR FEELINGS.

Brandy was shocked when I broke down in tears and admitted how much her behavior hurt my feelings. "Yes, I have tender feelings, just like you do," I told her. Knowing I was vulnerable helped Brandy see me more as a human being rather than the perfect mother who always had things under control.

7.
LET THEM KNOW WHOM YOU SERVE.

God has entrusted me with the very important job of parenting my teenagers. My decisions are based on what I think is the best choice.

8.
PRAISE IS SO IMPORTANT.

Kids need praise 90 percent of the time and criticism 10 percent of the time.

9.
LOVE SPOKEN IS AS IMPORTANT AS LOVE SHOWN.

At least once a day I tell Matthew I love him. At least once a day I hug Matthew. Even if we're at odds with each other, I do those two things with my teenage son every single day. Boy, is it tough some days! But such a commitment has softened our hearts toward each other after a disagreement.

10.
TALKING ABOUT YOUR OWN FEELINGS WILL HELP TEENS TALK ABOUT THEIRS.

Kids think that once you're grown up, you don't have emotional problems anymore. "You're mature, Mom," Amy has said to me more than once. "You should be able to control your feelings."

"Maybe so," I tell her, "but I'm human, just like you, and I need to feel appreciated, just like you. Let's help each other over the emotional bumps of life, okay?"

11.
LEARN TO READ YOUR CHILD'S MOODS.

I know when it is appropriate to challenge, discuss, argue, tease, and otherwise engage my son, Matt, based on what kind of mood he's in at the moment (and they change rapidly these days). This power of discernment helps determine how receptive he will be and how much of an inroad I can make. Sometimes it's better to table a discussion until later when he's more apt to listen.

Case in point: Recently Matt saw two of his friends fighting and broke them apart. One of the boys resented Matt's intrusion and stole a textbook out of his backpack and destroyed it. When Matt told me what had happened, I did not realize how angry he was with his friend. I "lectured" him about doing the right thing and told him that replacing the book was not important. I explained I could not call the boy's mother and accuse her son of stealing the book, since we had no proof. Besides, the boy had denied taking the book when Matt accused him over the telephone an hour or so before.

Because Matt was already so angry, my words only infuriated him more. He felt I was unwilling to go to bat for him and was letting the other boy off too easily. Life was unfair on all fronts. I was the enemy, as well.

The issue was resolved the next day when I was better able to communicate my feelings after Matt had calmed down and was ready to talk. I wish I had recognized the degree of his frustration earlier.

12.
HUMOR SENSITIVELY DISPLAYED CAN FORGE A FINE BOND BETWEEN PARENT AND CHILD.

Teenagers are notoriously sensitive—but they can still handle, and in fact, cherish, a few well-chosen teasing words from Mom and Dad. We also have a few funny nicknames for our two teenagers, names that we certainly don't use every day but just when the mood is light. And no, we never tease or use these names when our children are with their peers.

13.
REMEMBER THAT EVERY CHILD IS DIFFERENT.

Just when we thought we'd figured out how to raise a teenager (we'd had practice with our son Scott), along comes Natalie into her teens. What a difference! Many things that worked with Scott didn't work at all with Natalie. We had to start from ground zero to figure out how to communicate with her and get her to cooperate. Once we began to see her more as an individual rather than the ideal of what we thought a teenager should be, it was easier to assess her qualities and work with her.

14.
LISTEN, LISTEN, LISTEN!

It may be boring. It *will* take time. Teenagers need to tell you about their day. You may stumble onto a situation that needs a mom or dad's advice/correction/instruction. Kids will "serve" whoever praises them. Listen nonjudgmentally. Mostly, they are not looking for answers; they just need to discuss the questions.

15.
TEENS NEED SLEEP.

The growing bodies of teenagers require plenty of sleep. Since teens themselves won't always acknowledge that, parents must.

16.
DO YOU EAT TOGETHER?

We live in such a rush-rush world that, as a family, we hardly eat together more than once or twice a week. The refrigerator's stocked; the microwave works; we all know the phone number of the nearest pizza place. But we need more. We need to face each other—and talk.

17.
Don't Blame Yourself for Your Children's Choices.

Dave and I were not at all prepared for the changes puberty made in our lovely, sweet daughters. We thought that the problems other parents had with their teens must be caused by a less than satisfactory home life. *Wrong!* When children are babies, they go through the terrible twos. Then they grow up and go through the really terrible teens.

18.
Plan for the Best.

Plan for the best, but be prepared for the worst. Hopefully, you'll land somewhere in the middle.

19.
WHAT TO DO WHEN YOU DON'T HAVE
THE PERFECT CHILD.

People who have "perfect" children, those who follow your every lead, have no idea what it is like to raise a child like Jake. I have to be creative in my approach to nearly every situation. I pray like crazy, and laugh—a lot! Jake has his own learning style and personality bent. I'm still trying to figure out its angles and planes. In the end, all I can do is my best, with God's help, then stand back and watch the results.

20.
REMEMBER TO SAY
"I LOVE YOU" EVERY DAY.

My best friend's son was killed in a tragic accident—run down by a car when he was crossing a street at night. The day after the accident my friend said to me, "I forgot to tell him I loved him yesterday. It was my last chance to tell him, and I didn't do it."

21.
KIDS NEED TO BE SHOWN THEY'RE LOVED.

One night, when my daughter had three girls over to our house for a slumber party, I overheard one of them say to the others, "Ever since my mom and dad moved upstairs, we don't kiss good night anymore. I miss that."

Another girl said, "My mom and dad never tell me they love me anymore, so I don't say it back. It would feel really weird if I did say it, but I would if they would."

22.
GIVE EACH CHILD INDIVIDAL ATTENTION.

Every Saturday, for half a day, I have a date—with one of my children. Since I have four at home, they each get a Saturday in which we do what the child wants to do (within our finances). I'm a widower, and during the week my mother takes care of the kids while I'm at work. That means on the weekends they get my full attention. I make it a point to be truly interested in what they do.

23.
BE CONSISTENT.

Whatever image you portray to the outside world, especially at church, be the same at home, in your everyday life. Kids can spot the inconsistencies.

24.
ADMIT YOU DON'T KNOW HOW TO BE PARENTS.

My husband and I didn't have parents around when we were teenagers. (Both sets of parents were either dead or separated from us.) We had no one to warn us of the dangers or even to show us how to balance a checkbook. We want our teens to know that when life gets crazy around our house, and they're mad at us, they should remember we're doing the best we can. We don't have any parents of our own to go to and say, "Hey, Mom, what did you do when this happened?"

25.
What Did We Do Right?

When our daughter, Jamie, of whom we are inordinately proud, went away to college, we asked her how we'd managed to raise such a fine girl. She said, "You kept me in sports and church year-round so I didn't have time for television, drugs, or getting into trouble. You helped me get a loan for my car but made me responsible for paying it off. You always told me to be myself, not someone I'm not. I'm proud to have you as my parents."

26.
Start Talking To Them When They're Young.

When our older children were growing up, it was difficult to talk openly with them about life's issues. Maybe it was because my wife and I were so young ourselves. I think some of the problems we encountered might have been the result of not enough talk.

Our youngest son, who is fifteen years younger than the last youngest, is open with us about everything. I mean everything! He's fifteen. When I was marveling at this, I realized we started talking to him long before he was a teen. It was simple to do then as he was open to letting us know what he thought. Now, though, it's not as easy to get him to open up. But if we let him come to us and really listen to what he has to say, the communication flows. These conversations, I believe, are helping him make right decisions.

27.
KEEP IT SIMPLE.

Kids don't like sermons and lectures. Keep answers to their questions simple, short, and to the point.

28.
TEENAGERS STILL NEED CLOSENESS.

Until my daughter was twelve, I tucked her in at night, and we said prayers together. I don't remember a specific reason for stopping. Our schedule probably changed, or I felt too tired to chase her playfully up the stairs and into bed. I remember telling her she was big enough to say her own prayers.

Four years later, at sixteen, Cheri began pulling away from me emotionally. I thought it was just part of her being a teenager, but as our relationship and her behavior worsened, I began to look for ways to rebuild the closeness we once had shared. I started checking in on her before she went to sleep. She was defensive and suspicious for awhile.

I tried to make conversation by asking how her day had gone or how her boyfriend and she were doing. I really wanted to protect her and tell her how to avoid making mistakes in her life. (I dearly wanted to send the boyfriend on a one-way trip to Siberia, but I bit my tongue!) I had learned from past arguments that what she wanted was for me to respect her and treat her as an adult even though she didn't know about or want the responsibility that goes with maturity.

So, I listened, but when she hurt my feelings, I let her know, in a soft, genuine voice. I made sure we both understood what the other was thinking and feeling. We cried together many times and eventually started to laugh together again. Even though she was halfway grown, she still needed the closeness only a mother can give a daughter.

While our relationship isn't perfect by any means, we are communicating, and, by doing that, we solve most problems before they become barriers.

29.
TEENS CRAVE INDIVIDUAL ATTENTION.

When my sons were still in elementary school and both played soccer on different teams, I would take one to Taco Bell for an after-school snack while the other was in practice, and vice versa. We had more than an hour together, and we talked about everything under the sun.

The boys loved having their father's undivided attention, and I enjoyed hearing what was on their minds. I made sure not to lecture but played the active listener.

This became such a popular activity that even after they gave up soccer, we continued our father/son get-togethers into the high school years. These times alone build a comfortable, close, open relationship. With our busy schedules of work, school, sports, and church, sometimes our brief conversations dwindle to a relaying of necessary information to keep the household running. I get frustrated just giving out commands.

But when it comes time to go to the Mexican restaurant (we've graduated from Taco Bell), this makes up for a lot of that. As teenagers, the boys still talk to me about almost everything, something I treasure. I don't want to be a father who doesn't know his own sons.

30.
SOMETIMES YOU CAN'T FIX THE PROBLEMS.

My children and I have been through many hard situations in life together: divorce, health problems, death, and drug and alcohol abuse, not to mention the emotional trauma associated with difficult things. I used to say, "Everything will be okay." I wanted them to know they would always be taken care of. I used to try to find the answers, so I could fix the problems.

Now that my children are teenagers, I realize more

than ever that I don't have all the answers. I can't fix all the problems. I can't make everything okay. The only thing I can do is to love them completely and unconditionally, accepting them through the good and the bad. I'm learning not to be so worried about the bad stuff that comes our way but to see what we can learn from those trials and to help each other know that we're loved through them. Attending a six-week women's Bible study on the promises of God has taught me to trust in His Word and to know He cares about my children's well-being. In fact, and most incredibly, He cares more about my children than I do.

When the storms come, I pray—and I trust. I believe God will never leave me without an answer if I ask Him for one.

31.
YOU'RE NOT ALONE.

Having a thirteen year old and a sixteen year old has given me a personal understanding of what causes healthy, active, scarcely middle-aged adults to grow old and gray. If you feel overwhelmed parenting a teen, don't think it's just you. We're all in this boat together— but you will survive, with the Lord's daily help.

32.
THERE'S NO GREATER LOVE — ON EARTH.

Although there are many agonizing trials raising a teenager, there are also those glorious, poignant, uplifting times when all goes well, when you are so happy together, so proud, so grateful, you can't find the words to express the feeling. When you and your child speak the same language, know each other's hearts, and "blend your love." When you know there is no joy greater than having a child to raise to the glory of God.

Then it is that you know the ecstasy of being a parent.